D0677648

Copyright © Circle Press

Circle Press is a program of Circle Media Inc.,
432 Washington Ave., North Haven, CT 06473

ISBN 1-933271-08-6

Book Jacket design by: Angela Rios
Book Layout design by: John Lilly

All rights reserved. No part of this book can be reproduced
without the express written consent of the copyright owner.

Printed in the United States of America

COMMON NONSENSE

COMMON NONSENSE

25 FALLACIES ABOUT LIFE . . . REFUTED

Cliff Ermatinger

Circle Press
North Haven, CT

Dedication

This book is dedicated to the members of my families - those by blood and those by consecration - who have taught me to find the humor in the most humorless diktats of politically correct ideology.

Acknowledgements

This book would not have been possible without the help and motivation of my professors and students. Thanks also to Charlie Mollenhauer for his tireless practical help, to Thomas Williams LC and Shane Johnson LC for their encouragement and insights. And special thanks to Elizabeth Kantor, the kind editor who approached this book with an open mind and lots of wisdom, instead of cutlery.

Table of Contents

Introduction

I hadn't even buckled my seatbelt at the beginning of a long-awaited trip across America when a middle-aged man sat down next to me. The plane was almost empty, and he was claiming squatter's rights to my armrest. As I looked out my window at 20,000 feet and climbing, random thoughts began to take shape in my mind: *How many of those people down there are truly happy? With so many wheat and cornfields, with so much open space, who says there are too many people on this planet? Does the guy in front of me know his reclining seat is grinding my kneecaps into a painful jelly?*

I say "long-awaited trip" because the flight itself, I had thought, would finally give me some reading time. I suppose I was looking forward more to the flight than to my destination: an operating room and four months with a hard cast around my neck. At least the flight out was going to be just me and a couple of books gliding over the open spaces where the deer and the antelope play. Or so I had thought.

I hope he's a reader, I said to myself, checking the thickness of his glasses and preparing to offer him something to read. But, as it turned out, my fellow passenger wouldn't accept anything I suggested. No books, no newspapers—nothing seemed to interest him. I even offered him my Greek-German/German-Greek dictionary, to the same effect. He just wanted to talk for a while.

His conversation followed the deductive method, going from the general to the particular. So when we had covered the socially obligatory questions and observations on weather, destinations, and birthplaces, and it came out that he was a scientist of sorts, I wasn't too surprised. I don't remember his name or hometown, but I do recall what followed.

"My only certainty is measurable and tangible reality," he said.

"Oh, you're a fundamentalist, then," I said with my nicest smile.

His body seemed to deflate, and he looked like he might not be able to eat his "bag o' peanuts." Believing he needed more help than I could give, I was thinking about reaching for his air mask when he emitted his reply.

"No, I'm a scientist. That means I only deal with concretes. I accept only what science can prove. Everything else is myth." He said this last sentence turning his face away from me, like a bored museum visitor who has just paid his respects to the shards of an Etruscan urn.

I glanced out my port-window and searched in vain but could find no faith in all America as great as that of my fellow passenger.

Impressed, I said: "So, you have this pre-scientific conviction that it has to be that way, yet you have no "concrete" or scientific way of proving it. If all truth is tangible, and science is true, then what color is your science? How much does it weigh? Has science proven that there is no reality outside of science? Which scientific test proves this theory? It seems to me that you have made an act of faith in science, elevating it to a religion."

What had been condescension was quickly becoming pity. It was obvious to my seat mate that I hadn't yet accepted science as my personal lord and savior. His glare told me he knew I was one of those techno-ingrates who are quite content to benefit from the advances of science, but cavalierly discard it when no longer of use.

Our conversation covered many points that high school students I've taught in Ireland, Mexico, Germany, and the United States have raised, albeit not as articulately as my fellow passenger, but with the same sincerity. In spite of my less-than-graceful introduction, I tried to behave myself as best I could. I gave up any hope of reading and enjoyed the conversation thoroughly as we flew from sea to shining sea. I learned a lot in that conversation. Above all, I learned that although you may not know much, as long as you know something—anything—for certain you can learn a great deal more. I believe my interlocutor "deplaned" (if that really is a word) with something to ponder, as well.

The perennial questions that my fellow passenger raised, and that trouble my students, too often receive no cogent reply. The answers to them have a lot to do with the questions I was considering at the beginning of that flight—about happiness, the value of human persons, and the meaning of crushed kneecaps. As I got off the plane, I realized that my post-operation rehabilitation time probably offered me the only chance I would ever have to attempt to answer those questions in a systematic way. And so it is that, with cast on neck and ibuprofen at the ready, I sit rigidly at my laptop and type out these lines from the syrupy-numb world of painkillers.

This little book offers what I hope are a few convincing answers, but it doesn't attempt to exhaust any theme. I've tried to address the problems that trouble my students—and a lot of other people I've had chance conversations with—and to rebut the commonly held fallacies that I believe keep too many of these folks from seeing the real answers to their questions. Since these questions deal with real problems, and the fallacies are part of so many people's daily reality, I have tried to find answers to them in familiar settings: overheard conversations or discussions on trains with people I will never see again. I've also had recourse to those things that make us what we are and stand before us as guidelines and ideals for a full human life: the interior voice of the human conscience, insights from a friend, the adventure of matrimonial love . . . and cable TV reruns.

The suggested answers in this book are not completely original, and I hope that they don't appear too dogmatic. That's not my intention. They are just fruits of that sometimes too rare treasure called **common sense**, which is for common use, a treasure that is discovered only after a lot of observation and a bit of reflection. I've learned a lot, too, by listening to other people.

I guess you could consider this book a kind of basic operator's manual for life. I don't claim to be an expert on life, but, on the other hand, I have been living for several decades, and I believe I'm getting the hang of it.

I think, therefore I am, said René Descartes.

Shortly afterwards, he was seen in a quaint café and, when asked if he would like some coffee, replied, *I think not . . .* and disappeared.

FALLACY #1:

You can never be sure.

What can I know? This seems like a rather obtuse question: we all know that we know something . . . we think. But perhaps after a few courses in philosophy—or a press conference by one of the spin-masters—it doesn't seem so clear anymore.

To complicate matters, René Descartes came along and told us we couldn't trust our senses. He wanted to re-create philosophy from scratch (big job) by applying doubt to everything. He appealed to the experience every child has had of dipping the seemingly straight stick into the water and seeing it crooked. Pulling it out, the child realizes that the stick is straight after all and that his senses have fooled him once again. *Just can't trust 'em,* he says with newfound certainty.

Convinced? Neither am I.

RESPONSE TO THE FALLACY:
Are you sure about that?

Isn't it interesting that Descartes focuses on the apparently bent stick, and doesn't doubt that there is a child who likes to dip it in the water? In other words, his universal doubt is not really all that universal. The child, the water, the stick—Descartes is seeing them all together: none of them is put into doubt. Instead, the whole of what he sees forms the very credible framework for one small doubt. In fact, Descartes pays homage to his senses by depending on them in order to set the stage for his original doubt.

The fact of the matter is that we cannot deny our ability to know without falling into a contradiction. To say *I cannot know* is to say *I know that I cannot know.* To say I'm not sure is also to say I know I'm not sure. Knowing that we can't say we don't know anything without claiming to know something isn't much knowledge, perhaps, but it's a start.

The word **philosophy** comes from the Greek and means "love of wisdom." It's not just a particular calling reserved for pedantic egg-heads. We are all born philosophers, and it usually doesn't take too long before children begin to show their true philosophical colors. Anyone who has children, or has had to baby-sit for a few hours, knows what it means to be assaulted with "whys" and "how comes" that sometimes seem interminable. This questioning does speak of uncertainty and doubt, but the very fact that we all ask questions gives credence to man's ability to know with **certainty**. Otherwise we wouldn't ask. We wouldn't do much, for that matter, if we could never be sure about anything.

The very fact that we want to give a reason for the validity of our knowledge—that when we ask whether our intellect is capable of certainty we appeal to that same intellect—legitimizes our intellect, and makes us see with certainty that we can have knowledge. By nature, every man desires to know; and this same desire to know also causes him to reflect on the validity of his knowledge.

Is it all in the mind?

If we were to call into doubt the mind's ability to grasp the truth, what instrument would we use? *The **mind**, of course.* But that's tantamount to saying, *I know my mind doesn't work and I shouldn't trust it, but I accept its conclusions*

So we must conclude that there are things that we can and do know. The experience of knowing is spontaneous and natural. Things exist. I see them, have a certain relationship with some of them, and know them. What's more, I exist and I know that I exist. I could go on to say that I know that I know that I exist, but we'll leave that for another chapter.

The real existence both of the **objects** that are known (a boy putting a stick into the water, or this sentence, or anything else you can see, for example) and of the person who knows (Monsieur Descartes, who sees the boy, or you, who are reading this) is a fundamental truth. If there is no known object, man does not have anything to know. If there is no person who knows, there is no knowledge.

Both the thing known and the knower are called "beings" because they exist. They simply are. And we can be certain of this.

I yam what I yam.

Popeye

FALLACY #2:

There is no truth.

On your avant-garde

A long time ago it became fashionable to deny the existence of the truth. Everybody who was anybody in certain intellectual circles was positive of the truth of the proposition that truth did not exist. Like the leisure suit, this way of thinking has come back into fashion, complete with that off-the-rack quality and synthetic fiber that gave it its original appeal.

Does truth exist?

RESPONSE TO THE FALLACY:

Is that true?

In the last chapter we briefly looked at man's ability to know. We saw that both the things known and the knower are "beings" because they exist. In the same way, all that is or can be known and all that knows is called **BEING** simply because it is.

If something is, then it should not sound so radical to say that it cannot not be at the same time. Although he may not know it, Popeye is championing the **principles of identity and non-contradiction**: Seeing himself in the mirror or being aware of himself through his own action, Popeye knows himself as he is and, at the same time, knows what he is not. He affirms what he is and, in doing so, he automatically applies the principle of non-contradiction by recognizing that he is not anything that is not Popeye—for example, he is not Olive Oyl.

It's all because of Hume

In our search for truth we are also confronted by a third principle—the **principle of causality**—that is, the principle that there must be a cause for everything that is or happens. This principle seems obvious enough to us and nonsensical to contradict. But it is of the utmost importance for us to recognize this principle and accept it consciously. We need to take to heart the example of Dorothy, who was a great crusader for this truth—as she went through Oz valiantly singing, "Because, because, because, because, because, because of the wonderful things he does."

Notice that if we didn't accept the principle of causality we would never say "Compliments to the chef!" after a large steak dinner. We wouldn't have much to say about anything, for that matter, because almost everything we talk about depends on the principle that everything has a cause. There is no escaping causality, regardless of how much some philosophers, like David Hume, want to deny it. Hume doesn't say what caused him to deny this principle, but I imagine he must have led an extremely exciting life since he could never know what to expect to come out of his faucet every time he turned the knob.

Identity, non-contradiction, and causality are principles—that is to say, certain rules—that guide our lives, and without which we would find it very difficult to get along. But **truth** does not stop there. We can use these principles not only to verify but also to increase our knowledge. We can go beyond them. If, for example, we couldn't get beyond the principle of identity, our grade school teachers would not even be able to ask what 5 + 8 equals. They could only ask, "How much is 5?"

... and nothing but the truth

But we can go further. With these basic principles, we are now sufficiently armed to turn to the definition of truth. The word "truth" can be used in three ways. In the last chapter we considered the child dipping a stick in the water. Regardless of whether or not the stick was really bent, the fact that the stick and the child exist is a matter of truth. This type of truth is the reality of the thing at hand. We can call it **ontological truth**. Things are what they are. Not too exciting at first glance, I know, but very important.

A second type of truth is a kind of encounter between the mind in the act of knowing and the known reality. Here we can say that the truth is organized around two poles: the **intellect** and the known object. When we make affirmations we are usually dealing with this type of truth, which we call **logical truth**. This is the act of knowing something, an immediate relation between the knowing mind and the object it knows. When I see that there's a boy putting sticks into water, then this relation takes place.

The third type of truth is a direct result of logical truth. From the relation between the mind and the object comes true knowledge. When I correctly declare that the boy is actually dipping the stick into the water I experience a **manifestation of the truth** in which I know some reality with certitude. At the moment in which I verify this truth, I may say "Aha!" or make other appropriate comments.

If we deny any of these "truths," then we fall into a black hole. When challenged with *Prove to me that there is truth*, we must admit that it is a little difficult to come up with a ready response. Most people have never questioned the truth. Asking them to prove it exists is something like asking a fish to prove that he's wet when he has never experienced dryness before. He's immersed in wetness, and you and I are immersed in reality. Just like a fish out of water, we're all goners if we step outside of this most natural of habitats.

To demonstrate the truthfulness of reality (or the reality of the truth, if you will) we will take an indirect route by first proving that its contradiction is impossible. In other words, we will see that to hold any other position than the position that truth exists is illogical.

We have already established that logical truth is an encounter between the intellect in the act of knowing and the object known. In other words, we can say with little fear of contradiction that A THINKER THINKS A THOUGHT.

But, just for fun, let's assume that Monsieur Descartes is right and apply his universal doubt to this proposition.

A THINKER—THINKS—A THOUGHT.

1. Faithful to our systematic doubt, we put the THOUGHT under interdiction, telling ourselves we cannot be sure it is real.

2. This systematic doubt gets uncomfortable as soon as we make it truly systematic. If the THINKER thinks of himself, which he inevitably has to do, is he, too, not another thought to be put into doubt? Therefore, the THINKER, in turn, must be discarded, just as we set aside the THOUGHT.

3. Now that we have been forced to do away with the THINKER and the THOUGHT, nothing remains but THINKS. But how can this be? It's like saying that there is fishing but no fisherman, and no fish. We cannot even apply Popeye's principle of identity to THINKS because in doing so we would be applying laws to something that has no **existential** foundation. And without identity what is the difference between saying "THINKS" and saying **"MOE, LARRY, & CURLY"**?

Ladies and Gentlemen, we have just had a brush with the death of thought. But there is thought, so there must be thinkers and things thought about. In other words, we have to admit that there are no acts without actors. And this is undeniably true.

Here we are again in reality.

What is truth?

Pontius Pilate, 33 A.D.

FALLACY #3:

There are absolutely no absolutes.

RESPONSE TO THE FALLACY:
Then your statement can't be absolutely true.

I know that you know that I know that you don't know what
you're talking about!

Jackie Gleason in *The Honeymooners*

FALLACY #4:

Physical-experiential reality is the only reality.

This school of thought, usually called **empiricism**, denies that the physical reality we experience has an origin in anything outside itself, and even goes so far as to put the acts of the **intellect** and **will** of man into question. It claims that real truth is found only in experiential or physical activity. In short, according to the empiricists, all human knowledge begins and ends in the **exterior senses.** Simply put, if you can't smell it or see it, it's not real.

RESPONSE TO THE FALLACY:
Then what does the concept of "physical-experiential reality" look like?

While we can agree that all knowledge begins in the exterior senses, it does not end there. Consider for a moment the very idea that "all knowledge begins and ends in the senses." How do we go about proving that principle? We learn things from seeing, hearing, and so forth; but what kind of a physical experience is the concept "all knowledge begins and ends in the senses"? There's a huge contradiction inherent in this empiricist thinking. It elevates relativity and subjectivity of experience into an absolute truth.

The empiricists underline the fact that all knowledge begins in the senses. So far, so good. But they don't stop while they're ahead. They go on to claim that all reality, the intellect included, is confined within the limits of the senses. While we know from experience that the knowing process begins in the senses—after all, the first things we learn are those that we see and hear—to stop there is somewhat half-baked. We all have another experience as well, the experience of intangible thought, ideas that we cannot measure or weigh. And from our experience of intangible thought we can **reason** further. Ideas are in the intellect in a way that's different from the way our senses experience objects. The intellect knows **universal ideas** (also called **abstract ideas**) while the senses experience only particular things.

Fish is brain food or fish is brain?

If I see a fish, I have a certain physical experience of it: I see its bulging eyes and notice that it's quite bald. If I hold it in my hands I have an even more intense experience of it: I feel its slimy scales and smell that fragrance that just drives cats wild. If I let it go back in the water and never see it again, I can still have a certain experience of that fish by remembering it. In a way—different from, but no less certain than, the way I held the fish in my hands—I still have the fish in my head as a thought. If the empiricists were correct, my cranium would be the proud owner of a brand new carp. But the fact is, regardless of my appearance and what they may have called me in grammar school, I do not have any type of fish in my head—except my thought fish. And not only the one I caught last summer. I can bring to mind just about any type of fish. This is what is called abstract thought.

We can hook this fish from two angles:

1. By thinking about the fish, the intellect has spiritualized it. In other words, it has stripped the fish of all its matter and kept the idea or form of the fish.

2. The intellect, in a way, has become somewhat fishy. Because of one particular fish-experience, I will have an immediate understanding of the concept "fish" if someone brings up the term in a conversation, although that person has not been properly introduced to "my" fish.

The intellect can go further than just knowing fish. It can even reach the world of immaterial but true concepts, **transcendental** truths such as **freedom**, **goodness**, **justice**, and so forth, which are not limited to sense matter. I can't claim to say that I have ever seen a freedom or held it in my hand. And while I've seen triangular objects, I've never seen a perfect triangle, in and of itself.

But what is the importance of all this talk about brains and fish and triangles? The point is that we want to see just how far the intellect can go. We have seen that matter does not limit it, as the empiricists claim. And since our intellect can get beyond material realities, let's venture beyond them, shall we?

Man is not mere matter, or he could not entertain abstract thoughts. After all, things act according to their natures. Purely physical things can only execute physical actions. But things, such as human persons, that are both physical and spiritual, can execute both physical and spiritual actions. This distinction explains why we're hard pressed to find dogs that paint still lifes of their favorite bones, or rats reciting epic poetry. Such activities wouldn't be surprising if these creatures were spiritual. They aren't, but you are. Your reading this page is proof that you are a spiritual reality, because you see ink on paper in a certain pattern and know what the words mean through a spiritual process known as reflection. Even if this reflection is immediate, it is still a spiritual operation that goes beyond the merely physical. The spiritual (immaterial) nature of the intellect has to be admitted. Man is above the animals thanks to this faculty, which transcends mere corporeal life. <u>If man acts spiritually, then he must have a spiritual nature, because things can only act according to their capacity.</u>

When I think of last summer's fish, I take it out of its limits in space and time and bring it into the present. When I recognize that two trout have something in common, I am saying that they share the same nature. I am capable of arriving at the "whatness" of things— also known as their **nature** or **essence**. Natures cannot be seen; they can only be thought of, and the thought process that grasps them can only be experienced by a spiritual being.

Leave it to beavers

As we have seen, man has a capacity to reflect. But beavers do not. A beaver might build a suitable house for himself. He might even repair damage done to his dwelling, but by pure instinct. Man, on the other hand, goes beyond **instinct**. He reflects, sees beyond his present situation, and can imagine things that have not yet occurred. Beavers do not build their houses and say to themselves: *Wouldn't it be nicer to put a throw rug over there and perhaps do my living room with beanbag chairs?* No, they always have made and always will make their houses in the same fashion. Man, on the other hand, can come to his senses and say: *This lava lamp and that painting of the five dogs playing cards have gotta go.* Man can reflect and go beyond physical experience to imagine other not-yet-existent realities.

Our well-intentioned but misguided empiricist friends might ask "What's all this talk about a spiritual intellect? We know the brain is material."

In turn, we ask, "If the intellect were mere matter, could the brain think about itself?" In other words, could we be conscious of our own consciousness? If I know something, I not only know that thing, I also know myself, and I know my own knowing in the process. But if the empiricists were right man would need another organ (brain #2) to know his knowing (brain #1). After all, an eye cannot see itself. And to know brain #2, I would need a third brain. This regression would have to go on infinitely, but as the empiricists would correctly agree, we each get one brain and must be content with it, for better or worse, 'til death do us part.

So our knowledge is not bound by physical space. We, like animals, depend on our bodies in order to know. But the very fact that we can recognize our own corporeity (which means spiritualizing the body, making it an object of thought) proves that man is in part spiritual and not merely corporal. The very fact that we can intellectually grasp our own knowing (which is not material) establishes that not only that we are capable of comfortably fitting all matter into our mind, but that there are no quantitative or qualitative limits to our mind's capacity to know both material and spiritual realities.

By "spiritual" we understand that being that does not depend **intrinsically** on matter, even though it may depend on it **extrinsically**.

In other words:

1. While physical sensation has to do with matter and particular things such as the particular fish I caught last summer,

2. the intellect, on the other hand, forms universal concepts ("fish"—not my fish or any one fish in particular, just the idea of fish),

3. and grasps the essence of the material thing. That means that through thought I can give the same name to the thing I pulled out of the lake last summer as to all other creatures that are like it. I recognize the nature of fish.

Intellective knowledge, which deals with intangible objects, could not be limited to matter, as the empiricists claim. In fact, it has to be spiritual, because purely material things cannot do spiritual acts. Our knowing begins with matter, but is not limited to it or dependent upon it. Yes, it uses matter as a starting point; but it goes far beyond it, even without realizing it.

If not, it's back to **common nonsense**. If we were to hold the opinion that there was nothing else beside physical-experiential activity, then there would be no thought. And if there were no thought, there would be no opinions to hold.

To be is to do. Blondel

To do is to be. Nietzsche

Doo-bee-doo-bee-doo. Sinatra

FALLACY #5:

Philosophy is boring. I should know, I tried it once.

Philosophy has a bad reputation, above all when it's associated with the caricature of those angst-filled intellectuals who worry if they exist, and then worry about the existence of their worry. You imagine them slinking around in musty used bookstores or sitting around in dark, dingy culture-vulture cafés. But it's not exactly like that—the cafés are usually well lit. Thanks to philosophy's bad image, even the most basic philosophical vocabulary is avoided as impractical, or pedantic. But the truth of the matter is that there's more to philosophy than that.

RESPONSE TO THE FALLACY:
Go on, try it. Impress your friends. Perhaps it might hurt a bit if you're out of shape, but it's fun once you get the hang of it.

What do honeybees, spelling bees, BBs, the JuJu Bees, and the Wankel rotary engine have in common? That's right! They ARE. Yes, there's no denying it, all these things have one thing in common—their existence. And that's the subject of this chapter.

Being is not only good to talk about, it's good to know, and even better to have. Where would we be without it? Before going any further in our destruction of fallacies and championing of truth we had better lay some foundations: Things are. But how can I know this? Because they are. On the other hand, I can say with every confidence that they are because I know that they are.

Isn't that simple?

Immanuel can't

You might think so, but there are those who deny it. Some say that although things may be, we cannot know them as they are. Immanuel Kant was one of them. Kant claims that we cannot get to know the "thing-in-itself," the "Ding an sich," as he called it. (By the way, if you say, "think I'm sick" real fast, you'll have a good idea of how this term is pronounced in the original German.)

We have already discussed our ability to know individual material realities as well as ideas. In fact, knowledge was the first thing we discussed, before we even got to being. But that was just because we needed to establish the credibility of the tools we were going to be working with, before beginning to construct. Knowledge isn't the first thing. Before there can ever be knowledge (certain or cloudy) there must be being. In other words, if we know, it is only because the things we know are. So our response to Mr. I. Kant is *yes, we can.*

Kant says there are two levels: appearance (what we think we know) and reality itself (unknown to us). But if reality is unknown to us, how can he say it exists? We must conclude that it is impossible to eliminate the absolute from thought—"absolute" meaning the presence of being in thought things.

Someone might respond, *Oh yeah, what does "being" look like? I never saw one.* I would answer that being is not properly an exterior thing, but rather an act that everything that is does. Although we cannot point our finger at being or put it under a microscope, we can get at it through reflection.

But we can

Being can be compared to spirit, and yet it is the first thing that enters our mind when we see something, anything. If, looking up into the sky, I see a passing object, before I can even recognize what it is that I see, I recognize that it is. I am constantly finding being: in the sky, on the bus, in and out of my house. It's all over the place. It even is the place. Being in general can be compared to the ocean. Getting up close to the ocean, we see the fish and plants; getting up close to being, we see beings in particular.

We can say that we are open to being because we know it before we know anything else. If we try to deny being and our openness to it, we have to deny thought itself. And any denial of thought is thought.

If our first step is to see individual things, then the second step is to pay attention to what is common to all of them. Only through this type of reflection can we arrive at being.

Having considered being in general only very briefly, let's now take a looks at different types of being:

Real being: Those things that actually are. Chickens fit nicely into this category.

Ideal being: Those things that do not exist in actuality and cannot exist in actuality, but only as constructs of the mind. Chicken lips fit into this category.

Possible being: Those things that do not exist but could exist, such as the eggs that my chicken might lay in six months.

So it's not all in the mind

It's important to maintain these distinctions. People who aspire to little more than sitting around in their PJs and watching game shows often find it difficult to keep it all straight. Whatever kind of being we're talking about, our mind refers spontaneously to what actually does exist. We can't help using real beings from our own experience—like chickens and lips—and putting them together when coming up with ideal beings. The ideal and the possible only make sense in relation to the existent. In other words, the first undeniable truth begins in existence—being—and not in thought.

"All of this is very convincing, but there is a problem. If we all form part of this thing called being, then aren't we all part of the same thing?"

We are all part of being, but as **individual** and distinct beings. John is; a tree is; but John is not a tree. What makes things differ is their nature. For example, what allows me to read and write and do things that human beings do is my human nature. A dog is capable of doing dog things thanks to his doggish nature, and an oyster does what an oyster does and can't bark or scratch fleas because its oysterish nature only allows it to do oyster things, whatever those may be. Nature is what makes something <u>what it is</u> while being is what makes it <u>to be</u> or exist.

This nature—or essence, as it is sometimes called—always goes hand in hand with being. If an oyster were to lack its being, it would cease to be. If it could change its nature, it might become a dog. Being and nature are two poles: each thing has a nature (what it is) and being (that it is). We should be careful not to think of being as cookie dough out of which little beings are cut. You and the rest of the existing world are similar and dissimilar at the same time. The forms (natures, ways of being) are different, but the being (the act of being) is the same.

Being is a good that everything that exists holds onto—or else it wouldn't exist. A strong argument for the essential goodness of being is our instinct for self-preservation: the fact that every living thing fears annihilation and instinctively seeks to hold onto its being. We can say that the most fundamental good is existence itself. All that exists is good at least inasmuch as it possesses being, since being is a universal good. Naturally.

If merely "to be" is good, then what about evil things, such as weapons? Weapons are for attacking or defense. It is the goodness or the evil of how an instrument is used that determines the moral goodness or evil of an act, not the goodness or evil of the instrument itself. Inanimate objects (weapons included) are morally neutral. A hammer can be used to hammer in nails or heads, yet the hammer itself isn't virtuous or vicious. There are no evil objects, only objects that can be used for evil purposes.

And now, allow me to present to you . . .

We are all participants in being, but, since we are caused beings, there was a time when each of us did not exist. We were brought into existence. So there must exist something distinct from us that is the source of our being, that being from which all things have received their being and in which we participate in order to exist. It would have to be an **Uncaused Being**. Without this Uncaused Being nothing would come into being. We have already established the reality of cause and effect. If we deny the existence of this ultimate cause, nothing could exist. All possible existents need a present cause outside of themselves in order to exist. These existent beings can remain in existence only as long as they receive being. Everything that exists, therefore, stands in need of being caused to exist. An ultimate cause, an uncaused cause, a self-sufficient being is a necessary being whose existence must be prior to and coincidental with all other existing things. Something or someone like that fits the job description of . . . God. In fact, if He were to appear one day and call Himself "I am Who am," it would make a lot of sense—given the fact that He must be an ever-present, eternal being. In short, He is Being itself.

Let's make a few distinctions before we go any further. We often use the word "being," but when we begin to think about its meaning, it can become a little confusing. Here are a few definitions that may help:

Uncaused Being: God, who was never brought into existence and gives things their existence, their being.

Being as an act of existing: this what all things do. Rocks don't do much more than this. But we can. This mere existence is the primary goodness of all existing things, which makes their every subsequent act possible.

Beings: things that are. Your existence is something that is going on right now because of the act of being, and so you are a being.

When someone introduces himself, he says his name. When we identify something, we give it a name or recognize it by its name. Without going into oysters again, we can say that we usually take the being part for granted and just call everything by its nature. But in the case of "I am Who am" we're contemplating the Being whose nature is being. Here there is no bipolarity or distinction between being (that something exists) and nature (what that existing thing is). Rather, we are confronted with a Something or Someone Who exists and is called "IS." The utter simplicity of God's nature does not allow a compound of being and essence because His being is His nature, and His nature is to be.

In other words, the Supreme Being's "what He is" is His "that He is". And if something's nature is to be, it cannot not be. Thus God not only exists, He's necessarily eternal. (*Caution to the reader. If this doesn't make sense from the start, that's a good sign of normality. These are concepts that require a slow reading, and a bit of reflection.)

Further, if being is good, the Supreme Being must be supremely good. This Eternal and Supreme Being is also called God.

God is dead.

Young Nietzsche.

And I'm not feeling so well, myself.

Older Nietzsche.

Nietzsche is dead, and I'm doing quite fine, thank you.

The one eternal God.

FALLACY #6:

God does not exist.

The Russians are coming!

When the first Russian cosmonauts came back after their jaunt in outer space, they dispelled the God-myths of the Western world. No matter how high they went up, they proclaimed, they didn't see God. A dark day for the believing world.

My brain's too small

The agnostics, on the other hand, recognizing that atheism contains a dogmatic element within itself, claim that no one can know that there is no God. But then they go on to say, as if it were a declaration of humility, that even if God were to exist, human reason is limited, and God the Unlimited can never be comprehended by it.

Here are our alternatives:

1. Granting that God wasn't hiding from the Russians, we can know with certainty that He does not exist.

2. God may or may not exist, but we can never be certain.

RESPONSE TO THE FALLACY:
That's right—in a way. It's more correct to say, "God is."

It is often argued that the "so-called proofs for the existence of God" only help those who already believe in God. Instead of making excuses, or belittling the human intellect, perhaps it would be more honest to give the arguments a fair hearing.

I don't claim to be giving all the answers to **atheism** and **agnosticism** here, or even the best ones—just a few that I happen to have come across, that stem from human experience and reflection. These proofs aren't going to provide exhaustive knowledge of God's nature ("what-God-is"). What concerns us in this chapter is to get to the fact of His being (the "that-God-is" type of knowledge). We've seen that God's existence *is* His essence, but we have to establish *that* that existence *is* before we can say *what* it is.

First, a word about the limits of human reason, and of human beings. Human intellect in the abstract, as a faculty, is infallible just like our exterior senses: it reflects the truth. Human beings, on the other hand, are very fallible. Our errors come from poorly made judgments during the reasoning process. We gather sense impressions, which are correct, but we at times do not use the information correctly, so that we make false judgments in the reason. The problem is not a faulty reason, but a misuse of reason. Humility does not require that we pretend human reason is worse than it truly is. True humility means accepting the truth without ideology or fear. Ludwig Wittgenstein (yes, that's his real name) says that to draw a limit to thought you must think both sides of that limit. Not bad. What he's implying is that it is not humble but rather arrogant to claim knowledge of reason's limits in advance. Limiting human reason means creating a mental "forbidden zone." Such intellectual Puritanism uses reason to unreasonably limit itself.

We, in contrast to the intellectual Puritans, are trying to accept and affirm things as they are, as we have perceived them, as they are manifest to us. In short, existence is our starting point. That's the way things are. If we decide that starting with the way things are is impossible, if we deny our ability to know reality, then there's not much sense in any dialogue at all.

But we're not just beginning with the pre-supposition that God exists, and then going through the motions of complex **speculative** thought in order to say, "See, I was right." Far from it. Beginning with other pre-suppositions, such as the principle of non-contradiction, the general reliability of our sense perception, and the principle of causality, and using the intellectual tools that we have, we consider the proofs, and then, with great satisfaction, we say "See, I was right."

But before we begin our dialogue with atheism, let's see what agnosticism has to offer us.

You better you bet

We should be grateful for all of the advances of science. We all enjoy the fruits of scientific progress: our lives have become much simpler in some ways—and more complex in others. But, while it may sound mercenary, the fact is that most of us use science for what it's worth and set it aside when its services are no longer necessary or helpful. Even scientists act this way. It's important to recognize that science's boundaries are not life's boundaries, that man was made for more than theory about matter. It is unscientific to maintain that science exhausts the boundaries of human knowledge. The human frontier can only be unlimited. Remember Herr Wittgenstein's observation. If we admit an intellectual boundary, we necessarily think of what's beyond the boundary, and in doing so we cross it. Our actual intellectual limits arise from the limited time and opportunities we have, but potentially the human intellect is limitless.

And the human intellect has to go outside the limits of science to confront the questions of ultimate importance for human life—for example, does God exist? Agnosticism may seem tempting, but under the surface it has little more substance than ashes. Perhaps it appears to be a plausible theory on paper, but man's life is not lived out on paper. After all, how do you translate agnosticism into practice, in your actual life? Agnosticism is a decision not to decide. And not deciding is a decision since in practice either you live as if God exists or else you live as if God does not exist.

At the end of the day, agnosticism is simply unlivable.

And trying to live it is not smart. Is it prudent to live as if there were no God, all the while knowing that He may exist? Living that way is living like an atheist, with this difference—your atheist house is built on the sand of uncertainty. The possibility that God actually exists can hardly be relegated to the pile of never-to-be-knowns. It's not a question about some obscure historical figure from the past—but instead about a historical figure from our past, present, <u>and</u> future whose existence will affect each one of us in an existential way. Whether God exists is not like some unknown scientific fact that, once discovered, has little relevance to our lives—some new species of crustacean, for example, found living at the bottom of the ocean. The question of God's existence is quite practical. What's at stake is not just how we live our lives, but the very meaning of life. If God exists, life has a certain meaning. If there is no God, life has a completely different meaning. Obviously. If God doesn't exist, everything is up for grabs: There are no commandments, there is no law outside of myself, there is no need to listen to my conscience—there's nothing to worry about except looking out for me. If, on the other hand, God is real, then there is a relationship between one's behavior in this life and one's eternal fate.

Accepting agnosticism as a theory is one thing; attempting to put it into effect causes a theoretical implosion. The choice that agnosticism is too timid to make in fact has to be made in our everyday lives. Before the possibility of the Absolute, no one is permitted the comfortable posture of neutrality, and the choice that we inevitably do make is ultimately made in our actual living. Our choice has certain consequences in this world. And if, in fact, God does exist, it also has eternal consequences.

Blaise Pascal was a successful mathematician but an unsuccessful agnostic. He claimed that one could never prove the existence of God by reason. Pascal went on to say that while there are reasons for and against, one conclusion is ultimately true: either God exists, or He does not. Since, Pascal thought, reason cannot decide for sure, and since there are eternal consequences that depend on the answer, we have to come to some conclusion. We either choose God and believe or we choose to believe that He does not exist. We must choose. But how?

"Make a wager," Pascal said. You can bet God does not exist and live according to your disbelief, but if you die and find out He does exist, you have lost everything. And even if your disbelief turns out to be well-founded, you haven't won anything. If, on the other hand, you choose to believe in God and then die and it turns out He does not exist, you have lost nothing. But if you bet on belief in God and, when you die, you find out that God does exist, then you have won everything.

Understanding the odds, Pascal made the wager and later claimed that he went from his willed act of **belief** to an acute awareness of having won the bet.

Ante up.

In the beginning . . .

Others, who preceded Pascal, claimed to be able to prove the existence of God through reason. Here are a few of their arguments.

Something exists. You do, for example. To deny your existence is to affirm it. You can't say *I do not exist* and expect to be taken seriously by any thinking person.

But your non-existence is possible. You might not have existed at all, and in fact you did not exist at some time in the past. To say that you and I are not necessary is no adverse comment about our worth. It's just a recognition of the fact that we are a finite, **contingent beings** or **effects**, and not eternal beings. (By the way, an effect is something that has been changed by something else, the cause.)

Therefore, you and I were brought into existence by something outside of ourselves. This fact about us follows from the principle of causality.

There cannot be an infinite regress of causes for our existence, and the first cause of everything that exists is what we call God. Not convinced? Think about who it was that brought you into existence: your folks. Who brought them into existence? Their folks. There can't be an endless line of folks, just as there can't be an endless line of boxcars on an endless railroad, since if there's no first cause, then there can never be a second cause, or a third, or a fourth, and so on. Without a first engine pulling the next car, the other cars can't follow. If the chain of boxcars is endless, what moves them? Something has to. A chain hanging in space has to be hanging from something. This is the principle of causality. The longer the chain, the stronger the first link, which sustains it all, has to be.

We can't simply explain away what is not visible with a cavalier, *Don't worry about that first link, there isn't one.* Believing that requires a greater faith (and a less reasonable one) than believing in the first link, or the engine pulling the boxcars, or the first cause of existence. To deny a cause to the effects we witness is to wish them away, or at least to call them into doubt. The effects are visible, and they point to a cause, visible or not. The first cause wouldn't be the first thing we believe in that's invisible. We believe in lots of things we can't see. For example, we believe in electricity, we believe in neutrons, we believe in atoms. From time to time we stake our lives on our understanding of these things, which we can't see. No one even doubts their existence because it's more reasonable to believe in them than not to.

Consider the existence of the world. Is the world an effect? It seems to be. We constantly witness change—which is the operation of cause and effect. And none of the causes that we see bringing about change in this world are self-causing. The world's changeability (or status as an effect) means that its cause must be found outside of the world. We can't get around it. There must be a first uncaused cause of our existence. And the existence of this cause must not be merely possible, but necessary. This first uncaused cause, from whom all other existences draw their being, must be limitless (because whatever could limit it would be above it), eternal (because whatever could bring it into existence would have to be before and therefore above it), and unchangeable (because whatever could change it, would be greater than it).

It's a dependency problem

Things are in movement, and whatever is moved is moved by another. If you're not convinced, try diving off a bridge and pulling yourself up from the water by your hair. It just doesn't work.

Still not convinced? O.K., try this.

1. Observation: Motion cannot initiate itself; it must be started by something already in motion. Self-causality is contradictory. Otherwise, you could have existed before you exist and brought yourself into existence. Somewhat difficult: I've tried it many times and failed miserably.

2. Implication: An infinite chain of movers is impossible, because then there would be no first mover, and there would be no movement at all.

3. So there must be a beginning, and the beginning must be free of being moved by something else. In other words, there must be an unmoved prime mover. This unmoved prime mover is often called God.

We can look at this from a different angle. The argument doesn't have to be about physical movement. We can substitute "make" or "change" for "move." What interests us here is to establish that things are not self-causing. To avoid upsetting physics students, we can refrain from speaking about movement in space and argue from the movement of affirmation. After all, to engage in discussion involves a kind of psychological movement to agreement or disagreement.

Anyone who engages in an argument about motion makes an affirmation, yet this affirmation is an instance of movement or change. In an affirmation a person acquires something new, he changes somehow, and has something, if only in the intellect and his immediate past, which he did not possess minutes before. This is the passage from **potency** to **act**. No discussion is possible without this movement from potentiality to actuality.

And things cannot be simultaneously in potency and in act at the same time in exactly the same respect, just as you cannot have something that is hot and cold at the same time—unless you make jalapeño ice cream, perhaps. Therefore, just as something cannot both be and not be at the same time and in the same respect, so too is it impossible that something be both mover and moved at the same time and in the same respect.

So motion cannot initiate itself: nothing can go from the state of potency to actuality, except if it be caused to change by something in the state of actuality. The cause must ultimately come from something outside it. So whatever is moved is moved by another. But there can't be an infinite regression of movers because without a first mover, we would have no second or third, or fourth, all the way down to the present. Therefore, there must be a first mover of all things, which is not put into motion by anything else. This first mover we call God.

So the existence of the world speaks of God's existence. Only God, as being itself, explains the world's existence since there must be something, which is not given being but gives being. If not, nobody can get being from any source. If we have being it must come from something, and ultimately what it came from must be being itself.

But this first cause is not just something in the past, which set everything in motion and stepped back from it all.

A carpenter made the chair in which I am sitting, and the world in which my chair and I exist was created by God. But the continuing existence of my chair doesn't necessarily mean that the carpenter must still be alive. So how can I conclude the existence of God from the existence of the world?

The world depends upon God for its existence in a way that's different from how the chair depends upon its carpenter. The carpenter put the chair together and left it; he did not give it being. He merely put already existing things (nails and wood) together. God, on the other hand, created the world out of nothing and conserves it in existence in every moment. Think of it this way: everything that we know in the universe is dependent upon something to exist. You, for example: as long as you have food, water and an animated body, you exist. This means you are contingent. You depend on other things in order to exist in the way a light beam that depends upon the flashlight for its existence. But not everything can be like this. Imagine all the things dependent upon being. If everything is dependent upon being for existence, who provides the being? If everything were contingent, there could be no beginning. Something has to exist unconditionally and independent of other things in order to maintain dependent things in existence. In other words, this ultimate cause must be the cause of itself (an uncaused cause, so to say). The necessary element, the principle that gives everything in the universe being, must be—and keep on being—independent of the universe.

So God continually causes the world to be by continually giving it its being. All things that are, are because they participate in Being which, as we saw in Chapter 5, is God. They constantly receive their being from God.

In our discussion we are moving backwards from effect to cause. If we took a walk along the beach and found footprints, we would naturally think of the person who left them. We use the same approach when we consider the universe as the effect of an ultimate cause, in this case God. Our discussion about God's existence turns on this idea of cause and effect, beginning with the effect and ending up at the cause. For the moment we are not concerned with what God is, but that God is.

Is society to blame?

Man is religious by nature. All ages and all cultures have produced a population whose majority admits the existence of some kind of deity. It is sometimes claimed that this religiosity manifested by man has been imposed by "society." But the fact is that men experience the longing for God even in societies that have systematically stamped out all access to religious instruction and worship. We cannot claim that this is something imposed on man from the outside, by society. The longing for God is within man himself.

Even in the act of denying God's existence, the atheist testifies to the universal awareness of God among men. He is denying something, something that he must repeatedly deny. To repeatedly deny the existence of something is foolish. Once, one would think, should suffice. I do not feel pressed to repeatedly deny the Tooth Fairy, fearing that if I stop, she might turn out to be true. An atheist might respond: "I'm not repeatedly denying God. I have done that once and that was enough. I am denying the arguments of those who propose God, not God." But his response only betrays that the atheist himself bears witness to the common experience of mankind, which he's attempting to deny. His unbelief isolates him from other men, who in every age have been believers.

We know that man has a spiritual nature. It would make no sense for us to have spiritual capacities if there were no corresponding spiritual realities for us to experience. It would be just as nonsensical as if all men were born with eyes, but there was no light. Why the eyeballs, if there's nothing to see? Man's openness to spiritual realities and the Absolute itself makes it unreasonable to deny God's existence. Why should man have this openness if there's nothing to fill it?

The intellect is open to the totality of existence, both material and spiritual. The potential capacity of the human mind is infinite, but its actual capacity is finite. The infinite God cannot be comprehended by the finite intellect; so we know God through His effects, not in Himself. In a certain sense, the agnostics are right when they say that even if there were a God, we could not know Him. No head is big enough to hold such an occupant, I guess you could say. But the agnostics are also wrong: we can know something about Him.

One thing we can know is that God is personal. Only the personal gives reality and sense to the world. The world is thinkable only because there are persons in it. There must be at least one person who desires that there be being and order within the world. That one person is the end and the universal object of desire for which all acting persons act.

Man is naturally an acting person. When we consider man, we think of him as an acting person by nature. If someone acts, he acts towards a certain end. If one acts towards a certain end, it is because he does not yet possess that end. So we can say that the acting person is not completely realized. But, while his actions show that he hasn't yet achieved his end, it's also true to say that man is an end in himself.

The merely material being, a slug for instance, is incomplete without its action. It fulfills itself by eating, contributing to slugdom by mating, and doing all the things slugs are supposed to do—until it dies and is no more.

Man, on the other hand, is an end in himself. He possesses a potentially infinite intellect and a **free will.** He is capable of knowing and loving himself, as well as the totality of being. Man has a capacity for the infinite and it would make no sense for a nature to be geared toward something it could never possess. Man's openness to finite being and infinite Being testifies to the existence of the Infinite Being we call God.

Order in the court

Thanks to our intellect and will (more about the will later), we human beings are free beings. Our every act is directed towards a particular end. But not everything in the universe has intellect and will, yet these things too, move with an ordered purpose. The stars rotate in harmony, the seasons change, our organs function in an ordered way to fulfill their purposes. But these things do not act of their own free will; they have not been ordered by themselves. But if there is intellectual order to the universe, there must necessarily be a universal orderer. His friends call him "God" for short.

Here comes the Judge

The existence of God can also be proven from the natural moral law: Every man recognizes things as good or bad. And everyone wants to be happy. In fact, our every conscious act is guided by our search for happiness. We recognize **good** and **evil** in one way or another, and we know that we should do what's good and avoid what's evil.

There is an unmistakable link between what we are as human beings who know good and evil and what we should do—and also between what we actually do and what we become as a result. Man's behavior makes for his happiness (if he does good) or unhappiness (if he does evil.) It is no contradiction to claim that our right to happiness is also our duty to do what is good.

Despite disagreements about what is good and what is evil, there is a definite obligation within man to do what he thinks is correct and to avoid doing what is evil. We all have a direct experience of this in the promptings of our consciences. The human **conscience** is man's most interior and intimate core, in which he has an encounter with a voice echoing in his depths. We all find within us a disapproval of things such as murder and adultery, and we know we did not invent the repugnance we feel for those crimes. We don't just spontaneously decide these things are bad. Instead, it is apparent to us that there is a law that precedes us, which also disapproves such actions. Even if we engage in activities that transgress this moral law—robbery, for example—we still testify to our disapproval of such acts by our desire that nobody rob us.

And so it is not merely a question of what I say I think is right. I have to measure up to an interior voice which presents me with a law I didn't vote for. The universal experience of guilt for having done wrong speaks of our fallibility and of the existence of a norm that is prior to our decisions, and even our existence. We call this the "natural law," and every law implies a lawgiver. In this case the legislator cannot be man. Man does not give himself his own nature: he receives it along with his own existence. This first legislative cause is also called God.

Consider the moral consequences of a Godless existence. If there is no God, we have no law that could constrain us to measure our behavior by reason, by convention, by utility, or by anything else. The denial of God's existence makes all human behavior morally indifferent and empty of value.

Burger King Theology: *Have it your way*

Arguments for God's existence don't always convince. I once taught a class in Germany to a group including both atheists and people who professed belief in God. To my surprise, BOTH groups shrank back from engaging with the classic proofs for God's existence. They practically refused to do the intellectual work to grasp the arguments, apparently satisfied that God's existence was purely a question of faith. They seemed to regard attempts to find logical proofs were something of an insult to faith—whether faith in God or faith in no God. I conceded to the class that it is not easy to come home from a long day at the office solving practical difficulties and then have to give the speculative intellect a workout. But, I argued, if God does exist, then what could be more **practical** than knowing that fact? No logical syllogism imposes a conclusion. Acceptance is always a question for the will: we ultimately choose to accept or reject any argument. Even in our unbelief we retain our freedom, and we can use the will to reject the intellect's logical and reasonable conclusions—just as a tightrope walker can decide he wants to be free of gravity's laws, and stop living his life according to them. The law of gravity is reasonable, but I can choose not to obey it. But if I choose to break it, the law remains, and the only thing I'm going to break is my bones.

I told my class I was open to corrections or improvements and asked them where the fallacies in my thinking were. Where had my logic failed? That wasn't the problem, it seemed. When I asked the atheists where they took issue with me, they said they didn't need any proofs because they already had decided that God doesn't exist. One man explained that he didn't need God in order to not become an axe-murderer, and that he was already a good citizen. All of the theists appeared most appreciative of this observation!

Before workers demolish a house, they secure the area and clear the building. They make sure nobody is inside before they do their dirty work. They determine without a doubt that nobody is in the house. They don't presume that it's empty. They verify it scientifically by going through the house. If we accept science and the things it verifies, then we should apply the scientific method to atheism and ask it to—so to say—clear the house. Before they can claim there is no God, the atheists should review the entire universe and verify that no God is home, anywhere in all of reality. To do this, though, they must claim knowledge of all reality. Are they up to it?

In the atheist's drama of life—and even for some theists—logic seems to be something of an extra and doesn't play any major role. Rather than a problem of the intellect, atheism often appears to be a problem of the heart: a failure to acknowledge what lies in our knowledge. If we refuse to admit what our reason can discover about God's existence, we can have life just as we would like, without any divine hall monitor to check up on our behavior. This insistence on absolute autonomy seems to be the most widespread reason for atheism.

In the nineteenth century, a German philosopher named Feuerbach came up with this line, which has been the atheists' most useful tool: If God did not exist, he wrote, then man would have invented him anyway, in order to fulfill his need for something more than what this life has to offer.

Really?

I know a professor who says the opposite: If God did exist, we would invent atheism in order to continue doing whatever we want. Can you imagine not being eternally responsible for your actions? No eternal, unchanging God who knows your most intimate secrets, who sees everything you do, even your nastiest thoughts and darkest deeds? Yet Feuerbach claims we invented this all-knowing, unchanging God who will demand a strict accounting of our behavior on Judgment Day just "to make things easier for us"?

Nein, danke.

Extreme measures

I used to work on a loading dock with a young man who denied there was a God. Our discussions were rather one-sided, as I was trying to discover where his difficulty lay. I listened more than I spoke. He denied God's existence on the grounds that he simply didn't need God.

Finally, one day while out on a delivery run through the city, we passed by a seedy punk bar.

"That place is evil," he said with disgust.

I saw my chance. (Finally those philosophy courses were going to pay off.) "Sorry, you can't say that."

"What do you mean, I can't say that?" he asked with some surprise.

"You have been denying absolute goodness all along and now you claim to be able to recognize evil. That's illogical. By what standard do you judge anything to be evil? You have denied God's existence. Therefore, there is no standard outside of man by which you can judge things good, better, or worse. Such relative measurements require an absolute measure.

"Try to tell me the temperature with a thermometer that has no numbers, no beginning or end. You can guess, but since you don't know where you're beginning from, you don't know where you are. You have taken the absolute away. So too, among existing things there are things which are more good and less good. But "more" and "less" are measured by a maximum of good, the absolute standard. And you've denied the existence of that absolute good.

"We can't call things "evil" or "good" if we have taken absolute good away. There's no way to assess things without an absolute standard."

At that point in the conversation, my co-worker told me to shut up, and I did, since this stuff was aggravating him. I felt it was doing more than aggravating him, though.

We never returned to the subject until I left that job. On my last day he said to me, "I don't know who's right or wrong, but if you're right, I'll need a lot of help on Judgment Day. Would you pray for me?"

"Of course." And I still do.

Are you a good witch or a bad witch?

Question put to Dorothy while

being interrogated by the local authorities.

Date unknown.

FALLACY #7:

Isn't it a contradiction to say "God is good" when we see so much evil in the world—I mean with so many wars, famines, plagues, and whaling, and everything?

If God allows so much evil, He must want it. Therefore He's nasty. Or perhaps He doesn't want it but is powerless to stop it. So He's not omnipotent. Or, worst of all, He doesn't care and even if He did He couldn't do anything about it. Therefore He's nasty and weak. In any case, the God you talk about seems to be contradicted by so many tragic real-life situations.

RESPONSE TO THE FALLACY:
No.

This question has never been an easy one, and it is still more difficult to answer in the face of a real tragedy. The experience of evil in the form of suffering seems to be essential to the nature of man. Can any one of us say that he has been spared all suffering? The experience of suffering seems to be as deep as man himself, above all because it manifests in its own way a depth which would otherwise remain hidden to man. Suffering seems to belong to man's transcendence: it is something in which man is in a certain sense destined to go beyond himself—and he is called to this in a mysterious way.

A short time ago I was having dinner with some friends and they told me the story of how their seven-year-old cousin had died the week before in a car accident. Their question was how a good God could allow this to happen. It is a valid question that merits something more than a logical syllogism in answer to it. At the same time, life's tragedies are no reason to abandon logic altogether. Yet many people do just that when faced with horrible suffering—above all, with the suffering of the innocent. This chapter does not present an exhaustive treatise on **evil**; it simply examines the irrationality of rejecting God's existence on account of it.

Moths in God's closet

Before we turn to the different kinds of evil that we find in the world, it is necessary to point out that evil is not a being, nor does it possess being. There is no such thing as "an evil" in the sense of something that has evil as its nature. People mistakenly claim that moths eat holes in cloth. Not so. Moths would end up hungrier than they were when they started if they just ate holes. Moths eat cloth, and their meals produce holes in the cloth. Evil is like a hole in goodness; it's a lack of a goodness that should be there. What is blindness, after all?

A lack of vision. What is sickness? A lack of health. In other words, to speak of evil is to speak of disorder and imperfection. The majority of the fallacies on the subject of evil arise when we think of evil as something that exists, and not as a way of saying that something is missing that ought to be there. Evil has no substantial reality.

Three important truths about evil:

1. Evil itself is a nonexistence: something is missing that should be there. So it is not a real existing thing.

2. Evil exists in real things. In other words, something (a **subject**) suffers a lack (evil), but the thing in which the evil subsists, as something real, is good in itself.

3. Nonetheless, we often think of this lack as a real, existing thing. Deafness is not so much something as a lack of something: the faculties necessary to hear. Still we often speak of deafness, blindness, and so forth as existing things in themselves.

Evil is contrary to the nature of the thing it subsists in. Deafness can be thought of as a tendency that opposes or destroys the good of the ear.

There are evil acts, evil plans, evil choices, and so forth, but such things belong to a will that, though ordered to do good, has gone awry and is now disposed to do wrong. Bad intentions are to the soul what bad hearing is to the ear.

My exemplary big toe and the evil of pain

For example, imagine I accidentally cut my toe off while mowing the lawn. While I'm writhing on the grass making a spectacle of myself in front of the neighbors, the next door neighbor's son, who happens to have studied the problem of evil in a college philosophy class, comes over to tell me that evil doesn't exist. Instead there are certain priva-tions, such as the absence of my toe from my foot. Although his expla-nation is not very consoling to me, he is correct. If, while I'm lying there, I push the lawn mower in the direction of his feet as a token of gratitude for his timely philosophy lesson, I do not demonstrate that I am evil by nature; instead, I commit an evil act and become a morally evil person. Although I become a bad person, I am still a person who, nonetheless, participates in good because I exist. But the goodness of my being is probably not very consoling to him.

In this example there are two different kinds of evil: the pain felt in my foot and the morally evil act I commit by trying to inflict some-thing similar on my neighbor's son.

The first evil goes against my own personal good or well-being. It hurts, and without my toe I cannot do all the things I used to do. In the hierarchy of evil this is less evil than my act, for my toe suffers a physical evil, but my entire person is affected by my willed evil act.

Moral evil is more evil

Let's consider my evil act. Things are good because they are. The simplest kind of evil is the mere absence of good. But one of the goods that can be absent is the proper ordering of goods. So on a more complex level evil is a kind of disorder. Pushing a lawn mower is normally a good thing; it helps keep the yard looking nice—and if the yard is not mine, I could probably get a few bucks out of it. But if I use my freedom to cut toes off of smart-guy college students, my will is disordered. My will has mistakenly recognized something as a good for me (inflicting injury upon another) and has reached for it. The **moral evil** of my act is more evil than the evil of pain in that it does not merely go against my physical well-being but against the good of another man, against my own goodness, and most of all against the will of God. If God is the measure of all goodness, His will must be that we do the good. If I cannot now realize my physical potential as I could have with another toe on my foot, I cannot now realize my spiritual potential because of my evil act. I have frustrated my nature by committing an immoral act. To go against one's own nature means to contradict not only oneself, but the One who created human nature. And so a morally evil act contradicts God's will as well.

Just as living a good life makes a person good, so moral evil makes the person committing the act evil—while physical evils passively suffered by persons are not choices, and thus are morally neutral. In fact, experiencing pain and trials can be an occasion for great virtue. We define who we are through our acts and decisions. Robbers are robbers because they take things that don't belong to them. Even if some of them were to give money to charity, they would just be evil people who do some good things. When the will chooses to go against what is known to be good, it becomes morally evil. The demands of the moral law are unconditional, and nothing can justify their denial. In a morally evil act the acting person is always the loser because he denies himself what is fundamentally good and therefore becomes an evil person. God has written the moral law on our hearts, but natural law does not compel us to obey it. God has also given us free will.

God does permit evil, but He does not desire it. He has created us free in the hope that we will freely choose the good that He has made available to our reason. But even if we do not choose the good, even when we do evil, we should also recognize that some good can come out of evil, even if we can't always see that good right away.

There is no doubt that the death of the seven-year-old boy killed in the car accident was a horrible tragedy for all involved. The question is, why did it happen? Human freedom is responsible. Nobody wanted the accident to happen, but it happened nevertheless because of an error in judgment. If a driver made a wrong move, it was an error in judgment, freely made, though not desired. If a defective car caused the accident, then there was an error in judgment on the part of the person who put the car together or repaired it. It's not a question of uncovering culprits, but of admitting the truth of the matter: some mistake in judgment was made. God allowed someone to act freely even at the cost of this accident, without infringing on his freedom. God's permission allows us to act freely, but His permission is not necessarily a stamp of approval. This permission means that we have to live with all the consequences of our decisions. Our freedom implies the risk of painful consequences.

We need to be careful to distinguish the two kinds of evil we find in the world:

Moral evil (also called sin): Yes, God allows it. He has created man free, with the eternal possession of Himself through love as his ultimate end. If love is possible only through free acts, so too are hatred and evil. God is perfect goodness. He cannot cause moral evil to occur. Nor can He want it even with the intention that some good should come out of it. Any desire for evil by the Ultimate Good would be a contradiction of His very own self. Only creatures can desire evil.

Physical evil (also called pain): God allows it and, in some cases, desires it as a means towards a higher good. Augustine writes, "God does not interrupt our happiness on earth except to make possible a greater happiness after death."

If there is evil, then there must be a God

Regarding the denial of God's existence on account of evil: the mystery of iniquity is just that—a mystery. The entire context and ultimate consequences of suffering will always remain beyond our grasp. And our experience of suffering teaches us that regardless of the gravity and depth of suffering, rejecting God's existence does not solve the problem. Perhaps we do not have the whole answer, but the denial of God's existence is certainly not part of it.

To deny God's existence in order to solve the problem of evil is like cutting off your leg in order to do away with a sprained ankle. It not only makes matters worse, it makes the cure impossible. Some, however, follow this lonesome road.

Let's consider the consequences of such a choice; going back to my conversation with my fellow worker on the loading dock. If God is the measure of all goodness, doing away with Him does away with any foundation for goodness. Since evil is a lack of goodness, we would not be able to call anything good ... or evil, for that matter. In the absence of absolute good we lose our measuring rod for all value judgments and everything is reduced to **subjectivism.** Ultimately, taking God out of the equation increases suffering. Instead of offering a reasonable explanation to the suffering victim, it tells him coldly, *Your suffering is just a subjective emotion.*

Once we have removed God on account of suffering, man takes his place as the ultimate judge of good and evil. But if each man is the measure of goodness, who am I to tell a murderer his actions are evil? Isn't he, as a man, also able to define goodness? Why would my judgment be superior to his? The only way to do away with evil is by also doing away with good.

The existence of evil is a proof for the existence of God. Imagine a perfect, pristine world, which knew no evil or suffering. This imaginary world would already be filled with goodness and would have no need of God, since this perfect world itself would be god. Yet our world is not perfect and we know God exists because we know there is evil.

How come?

God alone, as the highest Good, can bring good from evil. It's only logical: I'm not offering some kind of placebo for suffering. God, as all-knowing, knows not only how He can bring good out of evil, but also the ultimate reason for it all. In rejecting the only One who can truly fathom this enigma, we reject any possibility of finding meaning in suffering.

At times we are made privy to the "why" of suffering. We come to understand the reason for the suffering, not usually through syllogisms, but more often through reflection and lived experience. I am acquainted with a family that knew little more than disharmony and strife. This family was at the point of dissolution until the birth of their most recently born child, who came into the world with several illnesses that confine him to bed and impede any speech. As the family members learned to accept the incurable condition of their youngest, they found that they had passed through a process of conversion. They forgot about their petty grievances and egotism and felt themselves drawn out of themselves toward the one most in need. Each one became a new person through this experience of suffering. The members of this family discovered life's fullest dimensions and their own dignity through self-giving. The child's daily struggles to master himself—his remarkable maturity and unexpected spiritual strength—have constituted a healing lesson for the physically strong but spiritually handicapped family members. This child's pain has been the occasion to liberate unhappy people and make them, of their own free will, totally available for the suffering person. In a certain way pain, in the form of a sick child, reconstructed a broken family and made a suffering boy the object of constant loving attention.

But the experience of suffering does not always follow the same pattern. Our initial response to pain is almost always protest, accompanied by a demand to know why. This most human of all questions will never find a satisfactory answer on a merely human level. Each child, each adult who suffers as the protagonist of some human tragedy is supported by countless other co-sufferers, in degrees according to their love for the one suffering. And they are all involved in a world of suffering whose profundity only God can fathom. These creatures of God suffer before their Creator Who, being perfect, could never be indifferent to their suffering—although we may not realize it. I continually encounter sensitive souls who have developed a personal relationship with God precisely because of their suffering. These souls, by entering into contact with God, by asking for—and sometimes demanding—an explanation for their pain, discover the reason in an indirect way. By becoming a sharer in God's life, the searching soul encounters much more than an answer to an inquiry about his pain; he discovers Him Who gives all of human life meaning. He discovers the One Who suffers for and with His suffering children.

I had the honor of speaking with a man who suffered the trial of Nazi occupation of his country, as well as having lived under a Communist regime. By the time he had reached his twenty-first birthday he had lost his entire family. Recovering in a hospital bed after having been hit by a truck, this profound young thinker named Karol Wojtyla discovered many things. Within the context of his own experience of suffering and through deep prayer, there unfolded a renewed relationship with God that provided him with a new understanding of what role God played in his life and how he was to understand his suffering. Still further, he discovered himself, his vocation, and his mission. His experience taught him paradoxically that through challenges and suffering man discovers his humanity in all of its dignity. Challenges and suffering are not ends, but rather conditions that can be used as opportunities to a greater end. The unlimited worth of man is best exemplified in man's triumph over obstacles, in self-giving and love regardless of the cost.

Every man is caught up in the complexities of a world whose imperfections often result from the abuse of human freedom. But man's capacity to rebuild is also a use of human freedom. It is, in fact, a higher freedom because in transcending suffering man shows himself undetermined by events and adversities.

Ironically, the question of why God can allow suffering is answered in love. If we have been created with a reason and a will, these have been given to us for our fullest possible development. Being free persons, not programmed machines, we develop and define ourselves through our particular choices and acts. God does not desire that we do evil, but He does allow it. If we were not free to reject love, we would not be free to love. And, as only experience can manifest, it is in loving and being loved that one becomes most human and, therefore, fulfilled.

While God's original plan is that we love one another and love Him, He recognizes that there is an inherent risk in the case of every human person—that he can reject God's love. We may not all embrace His plan. But it's clear that He thinks it is well worth the risk.

Once time travel was developed, the grammatical term "future perfect" had to be discarded because it was found not to be.

Douglas Adams

FALLACY #8:

If God knows the future, then we are not free.

It seems doubtful that many people really believe this. Yet how often have we heard it? We know it's wrong, but we don't know exactly why it's wrong. Is it prudent to decide life's most pressing issues on the basis of a sound-byte?

The consequences of this fallacy are interesting. If I'm not free, then I might as well do whatever I want because I am determined and I cannot be held accountable for my actions. But, if I'm determined, I can't do anything I want. Do I do what I want? Do I want? Do I do?

RESPONSE TO THE FALLACY:
I knew you were going to say that.

In order to properly respond to this fallacy we have to make some distinctions.

God's will: nothing more, nothing less, nothing else

Because they have intellectual faculties, spiritual beings have a will that can go beyond instinctive acts and make thought-out choices. Our experience of the will is that it tends towards its own good, which manifests itself in the **natural appetites**. But any tendency toward something else signifies a potential, something not yet completed. For example, when you're hungry your body has a natural **tendency** toward food. Your intellect grasps it as a good for you and, in collaboration with your intellect, your will impels you toward food. In the case of hunger, we can distinguish a clear lack: food. The potential here is toward a full stomach, the desire for which can be satisfied only through a not-yet-executed act: eating. In God, on the other hand, there can be no potential: since He is pure **perfection**, He lacks nothing. God is "**pure act**."

Who says nobody's perfect?

There is a perfect identity between God's being, intellect, and will. They are all just three ways of saying "God." If God is perfect, then His Will cannot tend toward something else for His own fulfillment, as created wills do. His will must be directed at Himself. Were it to tend in any other direction, it would be moved by something greater than He is, and nothing is greater than God.

God loves Himself because He is utter Goodness. God also loves all creatures because they exist, and their existence is the foundation of their goodness, which is a participation in God's own Being. God's Will brought all creatures into existence, and that existence is the beginning of their goodness. Knowing and loving Himself, God knows and loves all creatures as effects of Himself in the same infinite act of knowing and loving. God could not love us any more than He does; His infinite will loves infinitely. In this way we can say God is Love.

So God could not will evil even though he Has knowledge of it.

Time flies like an arrow (fruit flies like a banana)

Regarding time . . . Remember when we discussed contingent beings a few chapters back? **Possible beings** do not actually exist, but they could possibly exist. All possible beings are known by God. Although they do not actually exist, they participate in the truth through their potentiality to be and God knows them as possible but non-existent beings. Purely possible things are things that will never exist but that could exist through the power of God's willing act—since they are not inherently self-contradictory). We call this type of knowledge the science of simple intelligence because God knows these things with His intelligence apart from any act of His Will. For example, God knows that He could have given you a twin brother, but He did not will it. It is God's willing act (also called **adjunct will**) which, united with His intelligence, brings things into being: you, for example, and not your non-existent twin brother.

Furthermore, God is omniscient. He also knows an infinity of possible beings. He knows them in their essence to the extent that they could be or could have been. Finally, He knows them all at once.

No clocks in Heaven

As beings confined to space and time, we cannot help but think in spatial and temporal terms. In fact, our thinking takes time. We relate everything to the past, present, or future, and find this habit is difficult to shake off. That is usually where our difficulties with our freedom and God's omniscience arise. God is eternal, and therefore His thinking has a different mode, an eternal mode that consists in being simultaneous without succession. God does not think linearly or in syllogisms; everything is present to Him in one eternal knowing act. There is no future for God, and thus there is no conflict between divine knowledge and human freedom.

When we say that God knows what is going to happen, we are speaking in our own temporal terms. God does not see things as about to happen or as just having occurred. Instead, He sees things—even the things that are still in the future, from our time-bound point of view—simply as being.

Evil is not properly a thing. It is a kind of privation or disordering of a good. God knows both the good and the evil that is dependent upon the good and is unknowable any other way than as a lack or disorder in the existing subject. Evil can only be known in relation to the good. God knows evil because He knows good—just as we "see" shadows, which are really just places where there isn't light, along with light.

God is the cause of all that is good, and it is only in the good that evil can be known. God does not cause evil. Nor does He have foresight of it. All of our free acts are present to God the Creator in one thought outside the created restrictions of time, which He created.

Further, it should be said that knowing something doesn't mean making it happen. Even in the context of human limitations of time and space, we can see that our memory of things that are past does not affect the freedom of the things we remember.   In just the same way, the knowledge of future things does not limit the freedom of future action. The fact that God knows events that will occur does not mean that He has determined or willed them, merely that He knows the future. God knows what we will do since the future is already present to Him. God's foreknowledge is as observer, not protagonist. His foreknowledge is completely compatible with our freedom.

If you want to know what God knows about your future—even your eternal life—all you have to do is act, and make that future a reality.

God on prime time television is like God in American culture:
submerged most of the time, emerging only as a guest star whose
appearance is rarely announced.
Jack Miles, "Prime Time's Search for God," *TV Guide,*
29 March–4 April, 1997, p.27.

FALLACY #9:

If God is all-powerful, can He make a "PB&J" so big He couldn't eat it in one bite?

God's power is called into question here. There are numerous other variations on this theme: Could He make a rock so big He couldn't lift it? Could He create another God just like Himself? Can He create square circles? You get the picture . . .

When confronted with questions like these we usually don't know exactly what to say. We shuffle our feet, scratch our head, make a sad kind of smile, laugh nervously, and change the subject.

RESPONSE TO THE FALLACY:
"Huh?"

Rather than seeking an answer, these questions, knowingly or not, point to God's perfection. If God's perfection can be called into question, His existence too, is in doubt. But have no fear.

Just say no

Actually, the proper response to these questions is quite simple. If God is all-powerful, it is because He is perfect. Perfection is the key. As a perfect Being, God could never will anything that would contradict His nature. If He were to do so, it would, in itself, disqualify Him from being perfect. For God to make a rock so big that God couldn't lift it would be for Him to introduce an imperfection into His own nature: He would no longer be omnipotent. God wouldn't even consider such a challenge. He's above such things.

No "God, Jr."

But could God create another God just like himself?

This question stands outside the realm of logic. But if we consider it seriously, it invites us to go further into our knowledge of God. Until now, we have only discussed the "that God is" type of knowledge. Building upon that kind of knowledge about God, we can now get at the "what God is" type of knowledge.

Actually, perhaps a better way of expressing this is not to say that we are "building" upon the foundation of God's existence, but rather to say that we are approaching our knowledge of God's Being from various angles. Don't forget, God is not constituted of nature and existence, as we are. His nature *is* His existence. All the perfections that can be attributed to God refer to Being. The primordial perfection of God is that He is Being itself (or Himself).

God is simple

If God has no "parts"—that is, He is not a composition of attributes—so He must be **simple**. All creatures have natures. For example,
I am human; but I am not "humanity." I am a man, just one partici-
pant in humanity. In God, on the other hand, there is no distinction
between His Being and His nature. To be divine is to be God Himself.
While there can be many human beings, there can be only one divine
Being: God. He does not have any attributes; He is everything that we
can say about Him.

Pure Being is difficult to imagine. As with any idea we could have,
we must begin with our experience. The problem with getting to the
idea of pure Being from our experience is that we experience only
compound things. So we tend to start from compound ideas about
God, and then trim some things away: *Yep, God's so simple He doesn't
have any arms or legs—no hair, no Charlton Heston-like beard . . . just
about nothin' at all.* But we must keep in mind that it is not a defect
that God does not possess these things. On the contrary God doesn't
need parts to be complete because He's perfect. God's supreme simplicity is an infinitely perfect Whole.

God is perfect

Nothing can be found outside of God that would make Him more
perfect. He lacks nothing that he ought to have, and all the good that
we can find in any creature is found in God in its most perfect form.

God's perfection may be hard to imagine, but it is actually quite
logical. We are in the habit of speaking in a comparative or superlative manner: "My dad is bigger than your dad." The idea here is not
to prove that God is bigger than everybody's dad, but to demonstrate
that when we compare things, we implicitly refer to a superlative. As
someone's dad is said to be big, he more closely resembles that which is

biggest than does someone's dad who is a midget. On a **transcendental** level, we can say there are true things, truer things, and the truest thing as well as good, better, and best things. That which is greatest in truth is greatest in being, and the maximum of any grouping or genus is the cause of that genus, so there must be something that is to all things the cause of their being, goodness, and every other perfection. This cause is God.

(Of course, we only refer here to those perfections that are not limited or determined by matter, but rather are purely spiritual and express Being.)

Beings that possess perfections in varying degrees are not the causes of their own perfections because what one possesses of oneself, one possesses fully. If these beings possessed their perfections fully, we would not be using comparisons to describe them. And what one does not possess fully, and therefore does not possess of oneself, must be received from another. We cannot go on infinitely finding causes for perfections, so we must arrive at the Being who is all of these perfections in and of Himself in all of their fullness.

So God couldn't possibly create another Being just as great as He is. The mere fact of having been created would make him imperfect—and, therefore, not as great as God. Even to call such a Being "God" is a contradiction. And God cannot contradict Himself.

But this leads us to another question. Could there be more than one God?

No.

If that answer does not satisfy you, read on.

God is infinite

Infinite is an interesting word, a double negative that means "without limits." If God is pure Being, as we have established, then He must be actually, absolutely infinite. If God is pure act (without potential) He must be limitless. Since the foundation of the infinite is Being itself, God's infinity is not measured by the finiteness of other beings.

Thus, two infinites cannot exist. It is safe to say, This universe ain't big enough for the both of 'em. If two spirits were infinite, how could we distinguish them from each other? If one possessed qualities that the other did not have, then the other would not be perfect and, therefore, would not fit God's job description. If each possessed exactly the same qualities, then they would be the same Being since it is matter that differentiates members of the same species . . . and God is not material.

There is only one God.

Nature hates a vacuum.

Plutarch, Latin biographer (and moonlighting broom sales-
man)

FALLACY #10:

There's no such thing as human nature.

"What is man?" is a valid question—to which answers vary. Some hold the position that there is nothing in common among men: there is no solid definition for *man*. Perhaps, to some, it may seem a waste of time even to consider the problem. After all, if you have a good job, a comfortable life, and few concerns, the latest definition of man is not of much concern. On the other hand, if life is a struggle and you aren't financially stable, you wouldn't feel you have much time to listen to a philosopher's ramblings. *Who cares whether man has a nature or not? My concerns are real.*

It's a tempting thought. But consider the consequences if man has no nature. If there's no **human nature**, there's no **natural law** to follow. If there's no natural law, there's no objective good or evil. There's nothing stopping you from stealing and killing for profit or pleasure, or simply to have a new experience. Without human nature, human action loses all significance. The natureless human person becomes something of an intruder in this world, without any ability to establish relations with others. What are the others after all, if they have no nature?

No "Nature Boy"

Man, this indefinable mass, just exists and eventually dies. Everything between birth and death hasn't an iota of meaning, and all human action becomes morally indifferent. So what does this mean for the ordinary man in the street? There are no rules the wealthy businessman should follow, and the poor man is stripped of his human dignity. We merely exist.

Not exactly what you'd like to teach your children.

Yet Jean-Paul Sartre makes this very claim. He says man is a natureless freedom who has no orientation or purpose in life. And few philosophers had as much influence as Sartre in the second half of the last century.

RESPONSE TO THE FALLACY:
Then why use the word "man"?

While it is good to ask what man is, one cannot logically use the term "man," expecting to be understood, and then deny that term any meaning. At stake are the fundamental principles of man's nature. Consider the consequences of denying them. Remember, the idea of nature points in the direction of what things are and their mode of operating. And if we deny man his nature, we not only sanction moral chaos, we institutionalize it.

Doing what comes naturally

Plants absorb sunlight and water, drop seeds and die. Animals eat, sleep, mate and die. Before man dies, he can do a lot more than that. And when man does not truly fulfill himself, we usually compare him to one of the other two forms of life: avid T.V. watchers who lead a vegetative life are called "couch potatoes," rude men are called "animals," and moms complain that their children's rooms are like a pig-sties. In other words, one expects more from a human person than one does from pork and beans. Already we're seeing unspoken references to human nature.

It is in the nature of a dog to bark. It is in the nature of a cat to meow. We still do not know if slugs make any noises. Man, on the other hand, speaks and communicates. *But so do citizens of the animal kingdom,* you say? Not really. If I kick the dog and it yelps, throw the cat to the dog and it screeches, step on the slug and it goes "glitch," all of these animals are merely obeying nature and giving a response without any thought behind it. True, animals can respond to certain situations and reveal animal emotions like fear and hunger; but we never see them communicating universal ideas such as justice, freedom, truth, and so forth. Worker ants don't form labor unions. We can desire to "free Willy," but he will never give a discourse on his experiences in captivity. Man, on the other hand, has those same lower emotions, but also more noble ones. Man, even though he has a body as the animals do, can also discuss intangible concepts, and socialize with other men in a way that transcends animals' relationships.

If a body meet a body comin´ through the rye...

The most obvious elements of our human nature, common to all men, are all those body parts you and I have. (A physical deformity or an injury does nothing to lessen human dignity; we just recognize it as not normal—and that very recognition also argues for the existence of human nature.) Therefore bodyliness is a requirement of human nature; you have to have a body to be considered a man or **human person**. But it is only one component of the human person.

Human bodyliness goes far beyond simple animal bodyliness, because, inasmuch as it is human, it carries within it the interior vitality of the human **soul**. The human body is "human" inasmuch as it is interiorly animated (thus we call the body of a dead man not a "man" but a "corpse"). Human bodyliness presents us with the body and the soul together in an indissoluble unity: the man.

Human bodyliness is more than a requirement to qualify for "personhood." It is also the specific manner of existence of the human spirit: the body reveals the man, expresses the person.

This bodily expression is a manifestation of something spiritual in man. While man is a person thanks to his body, man is also a person thanks to his spirit. In fact the human person is essentially enfleshed spirit. When we discussed the intellect and its ability to grasp things immaterial, we came to the conclusion that man is spiritual by nature. Here, we can see that we can get at the "what" of things by observing their "how" of operation. If the human body alone is not a person, the human soul on its own is not a person either. Instead, the union of the human body with the human soul forms one individual person.

I'm a soul man

More about the soul: When we discussed the intellect of man, we arrived at the conclusion that it must be spiritual, given its immaterial operations. After all, as they say, *You can't give what you don't got.* The intellectual or rational faculty in man shows not just that he is a spiritual being, but that inasmuch as he is spirit, he is open to the unlimited horizon of Being. He is capable of transcending everything that is finite, including even himself. Further, inasmuch as he is enfleshed spirit (a soul united to a material body), he is finite, limited, and immersed in matter. In himself he cannot exhaust the possibilities of human existence. That means that, from the point of view of essence or nature, as an incarnate being, the human spirit is one among many: the singular man is one within a kind (genus); he is an **individual**.

Being a person means, above all, rationality, which is what distinguishes man from the animals. The term "rational" fits well into our definition of man since it is precisely because of rationality that man enters into the spiritual order. Many of the characteristics and dimensions on which contemporary philosophers insist when they speak of man as "freedom," "project," "vocation," and so forth are rooted in man's rationality. But those characteristics are not definitions for man. Nor are they reasons not to define man. Rather, each of those characteristics is dependent upon man's rational faculty for its very existence.

Here we must remember that it is the faculty, even if only in potency and not yet in act, that makes the person. Thus persons who may not have use of rational faculties—handicapped persons, sleeping persons, or unborn persons—are still persons.

Thus far, our description of man has hinged upon the concepts of individuality and rationality. We arrive at a valid description of man using these two concepts: the act of being of the individual and the act of the rational intellect that knows not only things, but the thinker himself, and his very own thought. Man is a rational individual, body and soul; and each man is unrepeatable and unique. For example, an individual's own personal experiences are things that occur only to that individual and cannot be transferred, try as hard as we may to describe them in their detail. You are you. An original.

Where there's a will, there's a way to define person

Implied by these two elements—individuality (self-identity) and rationality (self-consciousness)—is the will (self-determination).

From these three elements we can arrive at the absolute dignity and value of the human person.

It's not clear why **materialists** fear the existence of the human soul. They seem to be Flat Earth-lings in a spiritually round world, carefully navigating their way through life, afraid of what they might find. In denying their own souls, they affirm that they exist. But in denying their own spiritual nature, they strip themselves of their own identity and destiny.

If, as we have seen, the spirit is open to the absolute and tends to overcome all limits of time and space, then we can attribute a certain absolute character to the human person. Participating in the Absolute, which is God, man by nature is called to fulfill himself, to realize himself. Whereas Sartre claimed that a man makes himself, we respond that each man makes himself good or bad.

The human person, as a rational and completely whole individual, is an end in himself. By this, I mean to say that since man has an intellect and a free will, he possesses a nature that is open to God. That is, man as ordered to God is capable of coming into contact with Him and falling in love with Him. Being ordered to God is a necessary condition for man to be an end in himself, in that he participates in God's "end-in-Himselfness" through his capacity to know and love God. The invitation to communion with God according to man's open nature means knowing and loving God: the Absolute. Far from subservience, this is an invitation to human identity and fulfillment that can only be satisfied in God. Quite logically, if man is created with the capacity to know and love God, it seems only fitting that man was created with the fulfillment of this capacity in mind. True love desires the beloved, not as a means but as an end in himself. If man as a free creature of God is an end in himself, then human worth is such that no man should be considered an object.

That means each human person is priceless. He is non-negotiable and has an infinite value. Thus, as an end in himself, the human person can never be used as a means. This finality that man possesses is not absolute: rather it means he is an end in himself inasmuch as he is ordered to God. If man is spiritual by nature, then man must operate spiritually (the "nature" of a thing refers to how it operates). But nothing acts without an end. Man, being unlimited in his openness, must therefore be open to God. It is his nature to act in such a way that he will reach God, the Absolute.

Thus, a rational individual must be a being that naturally tends toward God. And each man is endowed with a free will to be used to achieve his goal.

According to an old Jewish saying, *If a human makes many coins in one mint they all come out the same, but God makes many people in one image, in His image, and yet they all come out different.* In other words, the sanctity of life is rooted in the uniqueness of the human person, in the fact that no one life can be substituted for another.

For who would bear the whips and scorns of time . . .
When he himself might his quietus make
With a bare Bodkin?
Hamlet, Shakespeare

FALLACY #11:

My body belongs to me!

It is increasingly common to hear the argument that one's body *belongs to oneself.* Thus are certain acts justified, which, according to this line of argument, would not be justifiable if it could be proven that one's body does not belong to oneself. Let's see if this argument should belong to anybody.

RESPONSE TO THE FALLACY:
Did you read the last chapter?

Lots of problems arise from believing we have things we don't. We have all probably experienced the embarrassment of thinking we have the correct answer and triumphantly proclaiming it in front of our class for the enlightenment of all, only to find, to our chagrin, that we were wrong. I've also had the burning-red-face-experience of arriving at the checkout counter with two shopping carts full of food, only to discover that I had forgotten to bring any cash whatsoever. I was positive I had brought money, and now I had to put everything back on the shelf or else leave it in the cart and try to make it home and back with money before the frozen goods became soup. The people behind me, according to their respective characters and virtue, were beginning either to laugh or to get angry with me. Fumbling through my almost empty wallet, I came across an unsigned check, which saved the day . . . though it bounced several weeks later. The moral of the story, I suppose, is that when you act as if you had something in your possession, which in actuality you don't, you either get hurt, or you get laughed at.

"Possession" does not mean "identity"

In a similar way, many people, for lack of correct information, believe themselves to be the proud owners of a human body. As their own possession, it can be used in any way they wish. Regardless of the many uses and abuses of the human body throughout history, a human body is not anybody's possession. The body is somebody.

We can consider the human body from several different angles. As we have already discussed, the human person is a composite of the physical and the spiritual. As a physical being, man exists in space. Being a human person puts me here and not there. Regardless of whether I decide to go to Hackensack, N.J., or Moosejaw, Saskatchewan, I'm here, wherever I am. I can't leave my body and still be me, nor can I separate myself from my soul. My body and my soul are myself, my very identity. My physical contact with the exterior world proves to me that I *am* physical, not that I merely *have* something physical. Ghosts walk through walls, but I have to use the door.

"Hey, that arm you just cut off me is gonna cost you $1.89, pal!"

When we say *my head hurts* or *my leg is broken,* we are simply locating the pain. Complaining about "my head" and "my leg" is more convenient than saying *my person is suffering because of a broken this or that.* It may help us to appreciate what is at risk here if we briefly examine some of the demeaning consequences of the "body-as-possession" line of thought. If we are willing to declare the body a possession, and not a part of our identity, then we should be prepared to leave all sentimentality aside and at least be honest enough to accept it at its true mineral value: a little less than a $10.00 market value. The downside of this position is that if a knife-wielding assailant injured us, we would not bring him to court for criminal assault against our person, but for property damage. Obviously, my body belongs to me, remember? How much would you get for an arm, anyway?

Further, reducing the human body to the level of possession nullifies any claims to personal rights. Property does not enjoy rights. Rights are associated with personhood, not property. If I steal your horse, I have not offended the horse, I have offended you. If animals had rights, then you could not own a horse or eat a hamburger in the first place. It's only because animals are possessions that we can buy them, sell them, and eat them. If we want to lower the human body to possession status, we have to be prepared for the logical consequences. *Bon appetit.*

I need my space

Californians may talk about their need for their own "space." But we should distinguish between types of space. When Mom walks into Johnny's room and calls it a pigsty, she means it's not fit for human habitation. There is a certain human relationship to space: space designated for human beings to live in has to be geometric space, but it also has to have a certain dignity. The physical space that human beings occupy has a relationship to human bodies, and therefore it has a relationship to human souls, as well. There is a dramatic difference between human bodies and mere physical bodies. A rock may occupy the same amount of space as a human person, but the difference between them is vast. The rock can be broken and made into lots of little rocks; the human person is an unrepeatable person, an exteriorization of something internal. Rocks can be thrown into lakes, onto roofs, off of roofs, and into holes in the ground or put just about anywhere without any moral consequence; but we all recognize that something is not right when that is done to human persons. Human dignity requires proper surroundings and treatment—which involve physical conditions, but which go beyond the mere physical.

Time is on my side

If I occupy space I also occupy time. Every thought that occurs to me is in relation to my present. I refer all events to what is happening now and say "before," "after," "late for dinner," "early to rise," and so forth. Human time is different from any other time, like that in which animals find themselves. Man alone has past and future experience. Soulless beings, on the other hand, exist in the physical world but have no experience of the world. In spite of the perpetual smile dolphins seem to sport (to be honest, I never trust anyone who always smiles), they, and all other animals, live in the world of the present—going from one sensation to another, never considering how much better things were back in "their day" or how they would like to spend their last days wielding a metal detector looking for lost treasures on the seashore, as we might. Time is different for man, because man is different from all other creatures.

Only man can appreciate the relationship of his body to spatial and temporal reality. Regardless of what time it is and where he is, man can recollect himself. Just as space can have a human relation, so too can time. In fact, we think of everything with regard to time. We know that every experience is unique and unrepeatable. Dogs just eat, run, sleep, eat, run, sleep and don't stop to think to themselves, *You know, this going after the ball gets monotonous. Who do these people think I am anyhow? One of these days I'm gonna snap.* They're prisoners of the present while man, existing in the present, can transcend it. Not only can man transcend time, he should transcend time. Man, existing in the present, is oriented toward the future and knows that his future depends in great part on his present. This is the basis for man's hope, and, being transcendent, man has the ability to hope past death.

It should be clear that the human body cannot be perceived as some object that has a certain relation with one's spiritual self. Instead, the human body and the human soul form one self. Human bodies are not mere objects possessed by human subjects: one can only possess what does not immediately pertain to oneself. One cannot commit the ambiguity of possessing oneself; one *is* oneself.

Author's rights

Let's look at this from another angle. There is a difference between saying:

A. "My body is of my being; therefore it is who I am," and saying

B. "My body is mine, therefore I possess it, and it is at my disposal to use as I please."

These are different, even opposed concepts. If my body is I, it cannot
be simply mine. I lack the ontological distance to appropriate it, and
make it an object for me, something that I possess. I can't distance
myself from myself in order to possess myself. It just doesn't work.

There cannot exist a human being without a relationship to corpo-
rality. A person is this human being here. Historically, there has never
been a human person who hasn't been at once a spiritual self and a
bodily self. Corporeity is the expression of personal identity that is at
the same time spiritual.

If my human nature is spiritual and corporal, then my body is not
an object foreign to myself, but my very identity. "My body" is not
"mine" in the possessive sense, because at my very foundation I am
not mine. Given that my freedom is not absolute, but rather a created freedom, it participates in the freedom of Him who created it.
Therefore my freedom is subject to certain norms and limits. On the
other hand, if I can say that my body is mine, as an object, I can use
it any way I please for any experience whatsoever. No law in the land
could stop me from taking drugs, from mutilating myself in public,
from any self-destructive act. Of course these things would not be in
my interests, but as acts they would have no moral content. Because
my body is mine. Right?

But it's not.

Would this absolute authority over my body give me author-ity over another's?

Self-inflicted violence or violence inflicted upon others is not violence against mere bodies, but against entire persons. This is important
to remember because the argument upholding abortion pivots on the
issue of the self-possession ("it's my body, it's my right"), which, so it

is claimed, would endow us with unlimited powers over our bodies. But, as we have seen, we don't really possess our bodies. Nonetheless, if our bodies were our possessions, abortion still wouldn't be justified. The aborted person who, according to this line of thought, has absolute authority over her own body too, is never consulted. Why this doublethink?

While I can say that I do not possess my body or my soul but am my body and soul, so too, am I a living person. Since I cannot claim authorship of my own life, I do not have the absolute authority to dispose of it as I please. Much less do I have a right to dispose of the life of another person, dependent upon me for its survival, such as a sick persons or a child, regardless of his location, be it in the womb of his mother or out of it. This is a fundamental law that no man has created, nor may destroy.

We will not be forced back into the "biology is destiny" concept that seeks to define, confine, and reduce women to their physical sexual characteristics. . . . The meaning of the word "gender" has evolved as differentiated from the word "sex" to express the reality that women's roles and status are socially constructed and subject to change.

Bella Abzug, addressing the UN, April 3rd, 1995

FALLACY #12:

The differences between the sexes are merely social constructs.

Mankind has had it wrong all along. A learned few have just stumbled upon the fact that humanity is not divided up into men and women; instead, we are a collection of five genders.

The billions of people who have existed since the beginning of history until now sure feel dumb.

A smallish group of cultural technicians maintains that sexual distinctions have come about thanks only to archaic mores and societal prejudices. In other words, there are really no differences between the sexes; in fact, there are no "sexes." Rather, there are these five genders: those born with male organs attracted to women, those born with male organs attracted to men, those born with female organs attracted to men, those born with female organs attracted to women, those born with either set of organs and attracted to both men and women. Unfortunately, the old-fashioned patriarchic manipulators have hoodwinked us into believing in just two sexes: men and women.

Our common confusion on the matter, you see, comes from a sick society, which, upon seeing a child and its genitals, corrals it into one of two parties: male or female. The child is dressed and educated according to its societally imposed sex-designation, taught to play with dolls or toy machine guns, taught to enjoy ballet if she is a girl or pro wrestling if he's a boy. In order to overcome these prejudices and impositions, women are told to pursue emancipation, to be like men and call all difference discrimination.

RESPONSE TO THE FALLACY:
If you don't believe in natural sexual distinctions, go live on a farm for two weeks and you'll see that not only are they real, but they are good, too.

Did Noah have it all wrong?

The recent campaign for recognition of five genders is interesting, to say the least. Perhaps even more interesting is the untold story of how those accursed cultural manipulators of old were able to convince not only all men and women but the entire animal kingdom to follow the same two-sex-charade as well. The bottom line in this debate is the distinction between the male and female sexes, which everybody has accepted until a recent few decided to have it otherwise. Instead of appealing to the fact that things have always been this way with no apparent difficulty, and instead of trying to respond to these claims with logic, we just need to look at the phenomenon of sexual distinctions which pervade more than just every human society—they're present throughout the entire universe as well. In other words, we need only to take a look, long or brief, and we'll see that all creation speaks of diversity and **complementarity**. Animals preserve their species through male-female relations, plant seeds unite with soil in order to give new life, and all creation sings the praises of this union of opposites which is not only the law of nature, but is life-giving and good. To think otherwise is to first will it to be otherwise. And that's not thinking, that's ideology.

Equality, or equal dignity?

There is a substantial difference between saying that men and women are equal and that men and women have the same dignity and rights. Obviously men and women are not the same, and therefore, not **equal**. Equally obvious is that men and women inherently enjoy the same value and dignity, something that accompanies them both throughout their entire existence, something they do not create or increase, but enjoy just by existing as human beings. This **equal human dignity** is not threatened by the fact that there are many things women can do much better than men and other things men can do much better than women. Very few women can pass the physical strength test to become firemen (or should we say "women firemen"?), while men paradoxically don't have as much pain tolerance as women but are usually far less sensitive than women. These strengths and weaknesses on both sides are results of something far deeper than social prejudices or even physiological structures. The school of thought that fears sexual distinctions especially fears differences that limit or favor. In order to overcome these differences, above all the ones in which the male appears stronger or more gifted, we are told to act as if they were constructs of male prejudice. Yet these differences are real; we can't simply wish them away.

What is most ironic about this mentality is that at its root is a very real male-biased prejudice that refuses to recognize what is truly feminine and holds up all that is male as the ideal for women. Women, according to this line of thought, should become replicas of men whether they like it or not. The male model is to be imitated, as if the female model were inferior or needed to play catch-up. This thinking also reflects a disturbing superficiality that refuses to go deeper than physiological differences, ignoring all the psychological and spiritual differences so apparent between men and women. Perhaps the greatest danger for women in this rejection of differences would be that a woman would find her dignity in what she does and not in who she is. This mentality, instead of recognizing the inherent dignity of each woman, suggests that a woman's worth must be earned. And this kind of worth is earned fundamentally through what is called "achievement in the work place" or "empowerment." The truth of the matter is that woman, regardless of her higher or lower position in society, her sickness or health, whether she receives all the respect she rightly deserves or not, finds her dignity not in merely what she does but thanks to who she is in her femininity and her humanity, both of which are inseparable and of infinite value.

Diversity and complementarity

We must avoid confusing the issue by superficially identifying sexuality with corporeity. Sexual duality is one of the fundamental data of the human being. The human person exists in two possibilities: male and female. Sex is a fundamental characteristic that accompanies the person throughout his (or her) entire existence. This **diversity** is found not only on the anatomical-physiological level but on the psychological-spiritual level as well, which is much more important. Man and woman are the two poles of human life, neither better than the other, but very much different.

These differences, from those on the cellular plane to those on the psychological-spiritual plane, prompt and orient our every act. In fact, just as we said in the last chapter that man does not have a body or a soul, here too it holds true that the human person does not possess his sexuality but *is* man or woman in the whole structure of the person's being. Man is man in his being, thinking, and acting. So too, woman is woman in everything she does. Think of the way we speak with one another: usually we conduct ourselves in a certain way with our friends of the same sex and in a different way if members of the opposite sex are present. Our social behavior has roots that go down deeper than social education. This difference in our behavior doesn't imply that we're two-faced, but rather that even on an inter-subjective and interpersonal level, our communication is partially but pervasively regulated by sexuality. The human person lives in an atmosphere shaped by sexuality and the natural, complementary differences between men and women.

Fundamental to the misunderstanding of the roles of man and woman—and perhaps even deeper than the fear of true diversity—is the hatred of **complementarity** that is so apparent in the radical feminist movement. To avoid this error, we should not understand **human sexuality** solely in the context of genital activity—or of any specific act—but rather as something that embraces the entire person in his self-realization, which, on a human level, is only achieved with the help of a member of the opposite sex. Matrimonial love is, above all, self-giving: man to woman, woman to man, and both to the children. This gift of self is something that has been experienced since man and woman first fell in love with one another. Complementarity is a fact and a necessity, not something to fear or hide from the neighbors, or to wish away.

Aside from the obvious physical differences between men and women there exist certain differences on the emotional level and even in types of intelligence. Certainly some stereotypes exist, but so do real differences. When we think of femininity an image of human warmth, understanding, magnanimity, graciousness, and temperance comes to mind. What is interesting about these feminine traits is that they all have to do with nurturing and keeping things within their right human perspective. While women tend to be more sensitive and aware of the needs of others, men usually are more self-centered. While women normally possess a strong sense of intuition, men are usually more speculative and discursive in their thought. These contrasts speak more of complement than incompatibility, more of needs and supports than conflict, for sexuality leads to the continuation of the species as well as the fulfillment of the person. Sexuality goes much further than any one function to bring about the realization of the individual as a person, with the necessary help of the beloved.

Where does this come from? Where is all this headed?

And so, with the complementarity of man and woman in mind, we begin to see what lies at the bottom of the "no sexual distinction" line of thought: an inadequate **anthropology**.

Absent from the "no sexual distinction" party line is any reference to the inherent dignity and value of the human person: male or female. The human person seems to be a type of raw material waiting to realize itself through powers or positions of authority and achievement. Success is measured by the personal desires for authority and purely material gain. Living in this fashion, one never seems to break through the most interior concentric circle of the "I"—to open oneself up to another in the act of self-giving love. If the radical feminists were right, how many women would have to consider themselves failures merely on account of having lived their lives believing themselves to be happy and fulfilled by loving and being loved, by giving themselves in love to their husbands and receiving their husband's love and forming a family, by raising their children to know how to love and live in accordance with their inherent dignity as human persons?

But these heroic women, and they are the vast majority, are not failures. They are the soul of this world, the ones who, just by being true to their femininity, raise and educate the entire world, and remind men who they should be as men.

What greater position of authority is there?

Alien to the "no sexual distinction" school of thought is any idea of true **love**, of authentic self-giving, of the sacrifice that every love requires. The five-gender proposal defines human sexuality (and matrimonial love which is the most exalted human relationship) in terms of unregulated sexual desire and little else.

Do we really want to go down that road?

•

Nowadays there is a tendency to claim that agnosticism and skeptical relativism are the philosophy and the basic attitude which correspond to democratic forms of political life. Those who are convinced that they know the truth and firmly adhere to it are considered unreliable from a democratic point of view, since they do not accept that truth is determined by the majority, or that it is subject to variation according to different political trends. It must be observed in this regard that if there is no ultimate truth to guide and direct political activity, then ideas and convictions can easily be manipulated for reasons of power. As history demonstrates, a democracy without values easily turns into open or thinly disguised totalitarianism.

Centesimus Annus, John Paul II

FALLACY #13:

I'm free to do whatever I want.

The writers of the *Declaration of the Rights of Man*, French revolutionaries and proficient aficionados of Monsieur Guillotin's objet d'art, believed that man should be free to do anything that injures no one.

Is that so? Are we truly free to do whatever we want?

RESPONSE TO THE FALLACY:
Not really.

Poor freedom. She sure has suffered a lot lately. Not only has she been abused, she's been misrepresented. She's been depicted as being able to do things she never dreamed of doing, and too rarely is she permitted the opportunity to truly shine, to do what she does best—to liberate and bring happiness.

We have probably heard the words *I am free to do whatever I want* more often than we can count. Those who say it are usually well-intentioned people, repeating what they have heard about man's autonomy and dignity.

Does freedom mean doing whatever I want to do, or is there a missing element in that understanding of freedom?

In the 1960s the movie *Born Free*—a story about Elsa the lion and her struggles in the African wild, most of which were caused by human beings, if I remember correctly—rode the current of the times, romanticizing the untamed and celebrating all that could be called "natural." I don't want to argue with the appeal of untamed nature, much less with Elsa. The problems begin when we attempt to legitimize something as good by calling it "natural" without a clear understanding of what nature is. We often treat the notion of freedom the same way. Recognizing that part of freedom means not being constrained, we call all restraints infringements upon our freedom and think of freedom as doing whatever we want to do. In other words, we identify the substance of a concept with one of its secondary aspects and end up with a rather confusing idea of everything.

Another difficulty with our understanding of freedom is not so much the confusion between the thing in itself and its attributes, but the belief that something is so just because I want it that way. There is a popular myth making the rounds today that makes the person an absolute authority unto himself. Actually, it's been around for a while. It is in the name of this understanding of freedom that I am permitted to satisfy my desires regardless of whether those desires are good or not. In fact, whether they are good or not is no longer even a question: simply by desiring something, I make it good.

But can we really define reality by an act of the will? The only thing I can actually define is who I will morally be. To believe otherwise is to live in a fantasy world. Yes, our freedom is real. But no, our freedom is not absolute, and we do not make things good or bad according to our feelings, desires, or best intentions.

Physical freedom

When we think of freedom and recognize that part of it means not being coerced or hindered, that is hardly a definition for freedom. I am free, but I am coerced by reality's laws and hindered by its limits. I am not free to fly down the stairs; I have to walk. I might want to fly, but am not free to fly because my nature as a human person prevents me. I am coerced to walk or run or crawl. I am not absolutely free in the physical realm. This isn't unfair, and it's nobody's fault; it's just the way things are. Perhaps, in a moment of defiance, I might try to tell the law of gravity that I am my own man and nobody pushes me around with impunity. I shove gravity aside, spring gazelle-like into the air and begin my less than gracious flight down the stairs, breaking everything except the law of gravity. That's not real freedom. That's dumb.

Psychological freedom

While we are psychologically free, psychological freedom is also limited. We know that we are psychologically free because our mind testifies to it. We are free to add 2 + 2 and come up with 4. We are also free to make a mistake in our equation and get a wrong answer. But we are not free to accept 5,396,873.144 as the answer as well as 4, both at the same time. We cannot accept both at once; our prepackaging won't allow it. We might say we do, but we don't. If I insist on thinking that two different answers to an addition problem can be true at the same time, sooner or later I will find myself in a large building with very friendly doctors but very strict rules. That's not freedom either.

Physiological freedom

Just when you were thinking you had enough of this, just when you thought you still had some freedom left, you find out you're not absolutely physiologically free. I'm sorry, it wasn't my idea. Things just turned out that way. No matter how much you will your blood to stop circulating, it continues its flow. Your skin, that independent part of your body that just won't behave, escapes the authority of your will as well. It produces cells every day without your permission, it gets wrinkled sooner than you prefer, and it is almost out of your control. At least wrinkles don't hurt.

Taking destiny in my hands and making a declaration of my physiological freedom by attempting to stop my natural blood flow will also stop my breathing. And that's hardly freedom.

Moral freedom: Liberty or libertinism?

Present in each one of these little examples of limited freedom is a conflict between the will and the way things actually are. This can give us a clue to the fundamental error of the absolute-freedom theory: the notion that the will stands alone. In reality, the will is not sufficient to achieve true freedom—especially when it's in conflict with reality.

As vision is oriented to light and color, so is the will directed towards the good. It doesn't help anyone to work towards a good in ignorance.

I need to use my reason and first recognize what is good, before I can effectively pursue it with my will. Recognizing what is good is the job of the intellect, the second faculty of the soul, which is directed towards the truth—just as the will, the soul's first faculty, is directed toward the good. The intellect allows us to consider our motives for acting as well as the consequences of our actions. Our will alone is no guide to action, much less to freedom, but with the intellect we can recognize what is truly good, and with the will we can choose that good. Upon man's heart is a law inscribed by man's Maker, called the natural law, which manifests itself through the conscience. Man's dignity lies in his possessing this law. The quality of a person is defined by his following it. We aren't forced to be good or to be evil, we freely choose. Nobody forces us to obey our conscience, it's our free choice, and the well-made choice is meritorious because it was freely made.

In the **conscience**, man is alone with God, Whose eternal voice speaks to him. There we have a conversation not with ourselves but with God, Who—sometimes delicately, sometimes strongly—puts demands on us that may constrain our pursuit of what we desire. These demands of conscience don't arise just from my own opinions about what is right or wrong, but find their source in the eternal Lawgiver.

If life is a playing field and the will is the ball, then the conscience is the rulebook. Appearing in a football huddle dressed for croquet is kind of embarrassing. In order to achieve success, it helps to know the nature of the game, along with its rules. And even then, only after lots of practice will you become proficient. Victory depends on mastering the ins and outs of the game and knowing the best way to play aggressively within the rules.

Our intellect identifies the things we can do, contemplates our reasons for doing them, and foresees the outcome. And our conscience works as a guide to decide what we should do. Our intellect can see the big picture, so that we can get a good idea of what we ought to do by seeing what it is that we were created to do.

Perhaps the kind of freedom that most interests people is moral freedom. We are often tempted to think that freedom is a morally neutral affair, in which I simply attach my will to something, to anything, and do it. But just as man is not absolutely free in other spheres of his existence (physically, psychologically, or physiologically), neither is he absolutely free in his moral life. To discuss moral freedom intelligently is to define its limits. Rarely do we consider freedom as a means toward another goal, but it is. Understanding freedom in this sense seems to be a question of maturity. We can either whine about feeling fenced in by our limits, or else recognize our possibilities and make the most of them. We can see the limitations on our moral freedom as channels and sure guides towards our ultimate goal: happiness and excellence.

Liberating freedom through responsibility

If freedom is the power to act or not to act, in accordance with the reason and the will, then you are responsible for your actions. Obviously. We could call no man good or bad if his actions were not free; these labels of merit or demerit reflect how responsible someone is in using his freedom.

We Americans love our freedom but often consider the responsibility part something of a party-pooper. And that's dumb. No other people has ever had so many delights with so few restrictions as we have, but the quality of our freedom cannot be reduced to the number of the options that come from this abundance. If we lack tools to choose correctly from amongst the innumerable possibilities, chances are we're going to mess up. Something is missing.

One of freedom's paradoxes is this limitation of freedom for the sake of freedom. In attempting to emancipate ourselves from freedom's limits, we end up rejecting objective and universal truth, which is the foundation of personal and social life. As a result we end up denying the only points of reference for choices about good and evil, and turning reality upside-down, believing that we draw truth from freedom instead of freedom from its foundation in truth. This is called **relativism**: Everybody is right and nobody is right. It's chaos, and we're living in the midst of it right now.

A relativistic society is, by nature, a provisional society. Society cannot last very long in a relativistic condition since such a moral cul-de-sac leaves no room for **moral value** or even a bit of the old *status quo*. Foregoing absolute standards for behavior, errant society begins to disintegrate, becoming a mass of individuals who consider other people as obstacles or, at best, inconveniences to their personal freedom. Each individual seeks to make his own interests prevail at the cost of mutual bonds, respect for persons, and common values. In such a society, what's valuable and true is decided by vote or force, and everything becomes negotiable, everything is open to bargaining, even life itself. Since the rights of another person apparently truncate my absolute freedom, and I create my own truth, what's to stop me from "fixing the situation" to suit me? When this attitude triumphs on a large scale, democracy goose-steps its way towards totalitarianism. The totalitarian state ultimately decides who has a right to life, what "quality of life" means, and who should enjoy it.

Individualism in the name of freedom makes freedom for the individual impossible. When freedom is divorced from reason and the natural law, it becomes a sinister caricature of itself and ultimately implodes. From the bloody holocausts of ethnic cleansing to the silent holocausts of social cleansing of the unborn and the old, the last century is a poignant witness to our excesses in the name of a freedom and rights divorced from truth and the natural law.

Let your conscience be your guide

A bad conscience meanders off the straight and narrow through ignorance or bad will.

Sometimes we don't know what we need to know, and, lacking the proper information, we can mislead and deform our consciences.

Or our consciences can become blinded through repeated evil acts. Our appetites can get out of control; then our thinking becomes blurred. In other words, we can allow the voice of our **passions** to shout down the demands of the conscience.

A conscience can be in a state of **vincible ignorance** out of negligence. A doctor who is worried about his golf game and doesn't take time to read a patient's chart may prescribe penicillin when his patient is allergic to it. He's acting out of a deformed conscience. Ignorance doesn't excuse him because he should have known what to do in order to get the information to make a good decision.

A conscience that suffers from **willed ignorance** is found in the person who doesn't want to find out what the truth is, because he knows that if he knows the truth he will feel obliged to live according to it. Believing ignorance to be bliss, he merrily goes his way with an even more deformed conscience than that of the negligent doctor, because his ignorance is willed—it's culpable.

A confused and scared young girl who is told to have an abortion by her parents and high school guidance counselor and goes through with it commits an objective evil, but under the influence of other persons. Her action is objectively wrong, but she may have little or no moral culpability if she operates solely according to wrong dictates of her trusted advisors. She could be suffering from **invincible** or **inculpable ignorance**.

But it doesn't have to be this way. The man who takes a little time and trouble to inform his conscience and find out what is truly good will find that his choices will be more intelligent and will correspond to the truth of the human person's dignity. Yes, the possibilities will be reduced, but that's no loss. In fact, it's true freedom. You waste no time on falsehoods and bypass mediocrity, going straight for the true and good. This is excellence. This is happiness.

Now you'll believe me.

Epitaph on a hypochondriac's tombstone

FALLACY #14:

Don't force your ethics down my throat!

People get defensive whenever the theme of morality comes up.
But the truth is not complicated. We are.

I remember the winter of my junior year in college. My college roommate was from Hawaii, so I invited him to come home with me for Christmas vacation since a flight to Chicago cost about a third as much as a flight to his home. Amongst the many sights and sounds that accompanied our wait in line to check in, I could hear a civil but serious argument between two passengers who appeared to know each other. One seemed to be saying that euthanasia was permissible, and the other was defending human life, maintaining that mercy killing simply wasn't right. Death's defender said quite angrily "Don't shove your ethics down my throat. Besides, how can anyone know?"

RESPONSE TO THE FALLACY:
They are not my ethics or yours, they're ours. ***Bon appetit!***

I didn't manage to catch much more of the conversation. About that time, our travel plans changed with the weather: the airline cancelled the flight. Some of the passengers complained and discussed changing airlines because the other pilots "weren't afraid of risks." Without an immediate ride back to our dorm, we decided to wait for some friends to pick us up and bought some burgers. The fast food place gave us our burgers in cardboard boxes instead of Styrofoam since paper is supposed to be more "eco-friendly." So that was nice. On the boxes were written the ingredients and, having little better to do, we read them as we ethically shoved the burgers down our throats.

I felt like one of the enlightened ones of our age. After all, how many people really read the fine print and know what it is they're eating? Then it dawned on me. There are people who do worry about how many carbohydrates they consume and keep track with vigilance. Others are not concerned at all. Others haven't a clue how the airplane they're going to take works; still less do they know if their flight is really going to take off. I found it ironic that we could have the most detailed information at our disposal when it comes to life's more trivial questions while in more serious matters we are willing to set the evidence aside in the name of expedience. Perhaps we claim ignorance of moral value in decision-making, using the words, "How can anyone know?" This seems to be a case of what people want (or don't want) to know, more than of what people really can know.

Excuse me, sir, can you tell me where I can find myself?

In the Sixties and Seventies it was not uncommon for young people to go to the Third World, to live in a Kibbutz, to travel Europe, or to join a commune in order to "find themselves." Many went out looking for a treasure never knowing that it was buried in their backyard all along. The fact is, we can go anywhere and join any group, but we still carry ourselves with us. Place and other circumstances are secondary. What really counts is how we live and act regardless of where we might be, for man is a moral being. Though at the apex of all creation, he is still a creature and, thanks to his physical body, has a rapport with those material things that surround him. Thanks to his reason and will, on the other hand, he has a special relation to his Creator. These relations with God and with other creatures regulate man's behavior, his moral acts.

Contempt for war crimes is universal. Just as universal is the admiration for acts of heroism—such as that of the man who, years ago, saved the lives of five airplane crash victims and lost his own life in the process, drowning in the icy Potomac River. This unanimity of reaction reflects something objective about morality and our judgment of moral acts. Yet we also have had the experience of divergence of opinion on moral questions. In our own dealings with others, we disagree on how people should act. What we call good, others call bad; what we would never do, our next door neighbor does with no apparent qualm. So, while there are certain things on which almost nobody disagrees, there are many occasions of dispute. Differences of opinion in moral matters reflect a certain autonomy of conscience and act. We are all quick to judge things good or bad, yet so few of us agree 100% on just what is good and bad.

We're not proposing any religious ethical system at this point in our inquiry. We're conducting our inquiry through reason alone, given our recognized ability to arrive at the truth.

All things that act, act toward their end. Every being acts naturally in order to fulfill and perfect its nature and through this process finds its own realization and well-being. Man, however, is the only creature that works freely toward his own **happiness**. Plants, New Age crystals, and animals will never be able to experience the happiness (or the sadness, for that matter) that man experiences. This happiness comes from full knowledge of the truth and from love for goodness. Given that God is the ultimate truth and goodness, man naturally tends toward God and there finds his happiness and true fulfillment.

Not by bread alone

Material things could never give a spiritual creature full satisfaction. Think of any material desire, and you always find something more desirable beyond it. Even if gluttony were our vice, we'd have to recognize that food isn't our ultimate end. The glutton doesn't want just food: he wants happiness and believes food to be a means to the deeper satisfaction he craves. Full? Yes. Satisfied? Kind of. Happy? Not necessarily. His longing and dissatisfaction will return with the next hunger pang. The same principle applies to any human activity. We always seek happiness by way of our acts, and as spiritual creatures destined to **immortality**, no passing satisfaction can ever give us ultimate happiness. The object of ultimate happiness for an immortal creature must be immortal as well—like God.

But what does all this talk about happiness have to do with ethics? A lot.

And now, for our next big act . . .

Rocks fulfill their nature by just being there, and animals fulfill theirs by following their instincts. Man, on the other hand, feels empty limiting himself to a couch-potato existence or living on the level of an animal, merely following his instincts (being a "couch slug," if you will). Man's acts are moral acts because he acts with consciousness and with freedom.

Human acts can be morally good or bad. But who decides what the criteria are in order to judge them? How can we know? The moral norm, like the treasure we mentioned at the beginning of this chapter, is not found here or there, but inside. Look at man's nature in order to discover what is good or bad for him. The good fulfills his nature, the bad deforms it or leaves it truncated.

When we take man's passions, instincts, and habits and also human freedom into account, we develop a better idea of what a moral act is. Our instincts and passions are full of energy and move us toward what we like and away from what we dislike. They render our freedom more difficult to manage, given the misjudgments that sometimes identify subjective "likes" with objective "goods." (Sometimes what we like isn't so good for us). When we let our passions get out of control, they can even blind our intellect, clouding our ability to judge precisely and act freely. It's impossible to stress too much the importance of our dominion over passions and instincts for the achievement of happiness.

When we speak of human nature, we should consider it in its totality. When we speak about what is truly good for man, we have to take into account the entire human person, in all of his relations:

1. Our relations with ourselves. What pleases the senses does not always have a rational end (consider alcohol and drug abuse, for example). Getting drunk may seem to be a good in that it is pleasing to our senses. But it cannot be justified by the intellect, which finds no reasonable good in drinking too much and thus determines that getting drunk is a wrong act.

2. Our relations with others (people and God). If we devalue others and only look out for ourselves without considering the well-being of others, we commit a morally bad act (stealing, for example). If we devalue God and try to justify ourselves by saying, "We're not hurting anybody: everybody is happy with the consequences" (dirty deals or kickbacks, for example), we commit a morally bad act. We may try to fool ourselves and claim that nobody is going to get hurt, but morally bad acts stunt man's spiritual realization.

Using your brain wisely

By using our reason we come to conclusions about the goodness or badness of our acts. This is a subjective norm and is of utmost importance. But we should not make the mistake of believing that anything we do receives its goodness or badness from our reason. Again, the objective norm is human nature itself; our reason simply recognizes, in light of that norm, that certain actions are good and others are bad. Our task is to use our reason to determine whether the end we are seeking by acting conforms to our nature. An evil intention can render a normally good act evil. If I decide to play my bagpipes, my act is an objectively good one; I am developing my musical skills and contributing *immensely* to the world of the finer arts. But if my intention is to play my bagpipes to earn money in order to buy and traffic drugs and black market goods, then I am committing an evil act. Circumstances come into play as well. If I have no evil intention while playing my pipes yet do not spare a thought for the fact that the intensive-care ward is not the right place for my musical prowess, then my would-be good act takes a nosedive.

Aside from the intention and the circumstances of the moral act, we must also take into account what is called the object of the moral act. Playing the bagpipes is an example of an act with an innocuous object, which can be good or bad depending upon the intention we have or the circumstances surrounding the act. But there are some acts that regardless of our intention and the circumstances can never be considered good moral acts. For example, we can never justify directly taking innocent human life. No condition or circumstance can ever justify such an act—neither the age, illness, nationality, or religion of the innocent victims, nor circumstances such as those in recent wars, when occupying soldiers have threatened to kill members of the civilian population if they refused to act as executioners to other innocent people.

Here we see an interesting twist on Sartre's belief that "man makes himself." Within the framework of moral life, it becomes clear that man does indeed make himself, but not in the sense of creating his own being. He makes himself good or bad through his own free moral acts.

Human dignity requires worthy acts

Some acts are intrinsically evil because of the incongruence between the act and the human nature of the one acting. This is an element not often considered. Most frequently we regard the innocence of the victim as the reason that the act is wrong, but we should also consider that if the act goes against the nature of the one acting, he is behaving in a way that does not become his human nature, and so his act cannot be justified. For example, an animal has no rights, but that does not grant me free reign to treat the animal as I please. Upon torturing the animal, I cease to act according to the dignity of my humanity and fall far below it.

So we begin to see the obligations that our nature puts us under. Our own nature is the norm for truly human behavior, and it is our own reason that recognizes what conforms to our nature and what detracts from it. Thus we discover that we must seek to do good and avoid doing any evil in order to obtain our end.

Are we to conclude then that the obligation to do good and avoid evil comes from ourselves?

Not really. Moral obligation could not find its necessity in man, for he would then be the master of it and, as master, could "unoblige" himself. Nor is it found in others, for no man could dictate to the conscience of another man. Therefore, moral obligation must be found outside of man and above man, for nothing below man could thus oblige him. The only authority superior to man is the author of man's nature, his Creator. God has not acted arbitrarily but desires that man act according to his human nature in freedom and avoid what is not in conformity with it. The ultimate foundation of all moral obligation is God.

The key to every problem is a principle, as the key to every cipher is a code. When a man knows his own principle of action he can act.

G. K. Chesterton

FALLACY #15:

You just admitted that there is a lot of divergence of opinion as to how we should act. Therefore, there can be no universally binding law to govern us.

How can we say there's a universally binding law if we can't agree on what it is? What was considered immoral 100 years ago is common practice today, and some of what we do today will be looked upon with horror in 100 years. So where's this immutable **natural law** you're talking about?

RESPONSE TO THE FALLACY:

The moral law is natural, universal, and obligatory. Whether we live by it or not does not change it.

While this is a good question that requires a well-thought-out response, the answer is not really very complex.

When we hear the word "law," especially in America, we start to get defensive and question its authority; we look for a loophole, a tax shelter. And if we can find no legal escape, we may decide to disobey the law and appease our consciences with such words as "I didn't vote for this law, anyway." This way of dealing with the law is one thing when we're dealing with law created by men, known as **positive law**. But this same reaction is a different thing altogether when the issue is the law created by God.

God's law does not refer only to **revealed law**, which we know through His divine intervention, but also to the plan He has in mind behind every speck of creation, the **natural law**. Remember how nature refers to what something is? Nature, then, is a reflection of God's eternal law. Just as it is part of God's law that heavy objects fall downward, regardless of who may have voted against it, in the same way certain moral principles are part of His law, no matter what Congress might say about them. In other words, all of nature's laws, whether those that govern inanimate objects or those that deal with morality, should be recognized as individual reflections of the one eternal law found in God's eternal plan.

Laws you didn't vote for

Every person feels a certain inclination to good and a certain repugnance for evil. These are universal. And man's dignity, which is affirmed by his intellect and will, discovers varying degrees of value attached to various things. Rocks are subject to God's law and have no choice but to fall downwards. But man's dignity is such that he is submitted to more elaborate laws and is free to follow them or reject them. A rock fulfills its nature by just lying there doing nothing. That's what rocks are supposed to do. To fulfill his human nature, man has to obey moral laws. But how does man know these laws? Again, look within man to see where he should go and what he should do: consider his nature.

Our nature is oriented towards what is good, so "do good and avoid evil" is the fundamental principle of the natural law for man. But what is "good"? As we have already established, our intellect and will are ordered faculties, that is, they are oriented toward certain ends, the true and the good. The most general expression of our search for truth and goodness is in man's tendency to hang on to some things with all his being. Amongst the things men cling to we find self-preservation: thus we know that respect for life is an absolute value, despite some people's defense of the "choice" to snuff out some lives. We also find a tendency to conserve and care for the human species: thus we know that marital fidelity and indissolubility, which are necessary for the care of children, are good. Further, the tendency man has to want to live in society implies certain rights and duties men must observe in their relations with each other.

But the natural law isn't limited merely to certain vague principles; man doesn't live on a theoretical level, but on a practical one. Basic moral principles have to be applied in concrete circumstances. It's up to the reason to judge what to do when we are confronted with values and anti-values, and then we must act in conformity with our reason, applying moral principles. Keep in mind that the natural law was written by man's Creator. Obviously, it could not come from man, or else man who made it could do away with it. It's imperative to keep in mind that we don't create values, we recognize them. We must use our reason to choose from among our options in order to do what is good and avoid what is evil in each concrete situation.

Using reason to decide between good and bad isn't a faculty we have recourse to infrequently. In every moment of our conscious life we find ourselves choosing between good and bad, or between good and less good. In the morning we choose to take a shower because we believe it is better to go to work squeaky clean rather than smelling like yesterday's dinner and basketball game. Regardless of the small amount of time we dedicate to the decision, it is a choice we make, believing we are opting for the better of two choices. We have a certain inclination to cleanliness, which reason applies to the situation to reach the conclusion that, yes, there are far more positive aspects to our going to work clean than dirty (even if going unwashed would guarantee us a section on the bus all to ourselves). Our more complex moral choices are similar. In order to be good and fulfill our selves, we must evaluate, judge, and act according to what is in harmony with our nature.

Hey, don't you go changin´

Since reason is essential to man and natural law proceeds from the reason, we can conclude that the natural law is universal and valid for all men.

Some may raise objections. They appeal to the obvious and wide-scale breaches of what we call the natural law: ethnic cleansing as recent as what happened in Rwanda in the 1990s and as far back as what Oliver Cromwell did in Ireland and Scotland, almost universal acceptance of slavery followed by almost universal condemnation of it, and so forth. Inconsistent and horrendous human behavior leads some to the conclusion that there must be no natural law. Not exactly a proof. Look at this type of logic (if we can call it that) another way. We have all experienced riding on the bus next to someone who smells somewhat overripe. But this phenomenon doesn't convince us that cleanliness should be tossed aside as prudery. In fact, such encounters seem to convince us even more of its legitimacy and urgency. The same goes for natural law. The very fact that we observe it being broken is proof that we recognize its universality.

Not *To be or not to be?* but *Just to be, or to truly live?*

While one cannot claim ignorance of the great moral principles, one can choose not to live by those principles. That's why we call some people "criminals" and build prisons to house them. They are people who have refused to apply those principles.

It appears obvious that natural law exists, for there is a series of things that are "proper" to man independent of human laws: life, body, soul, liberty, honor, the development of his faculties, and so forth. Equally obvious is the respect others should show for these things in a person, in order for him to fulfill himself. Nature not only indicates right action, it requires it of the person for his own self-realization. The natural law is the obliging force behind all man-made laws that conform to it.

Since human nature does not change, neither does natural law. The natural law is immutable both intrinsically and extrinsically. Actions that are just or unjust in themselves can never be good actions. If an action contradicts what is required for us to fulfill our human nature, it will always be against the natural law. And no one, not even God, can oblige anyone to do anything against the law of human nature.

It is false to claim that a change of custom, or even the general acceptance in one epoch of what is now considered immoral, refutes the natural law. It is true that every age has had its run-ins with the natural law, but no epoch has been able to cancel out "do good and avoid evil." While some things have changed, the majority of **moral judgments** have not: Murder, theft, lying, adultery, and a host of other unsavory hobbies have always been recognized as wrong.

Currently a type of "situation ethics" is in vogue. This brand of morality is founded on apparent differences in ethical practice, which allegedly indicate a certain mutability of moral norms. But situation ethics leaves aside all consideration of what man is and lends a certain absoluteness to the individual in his own decision-making. In other words, a human person is taken out of the context of his nature and is made his own point of reference for morality. But we know that what unites men is their common nature (in fact our sameness is what allows us to communicate with each other). Yet, in spite of a common nature directed by the natural law, some changes in moral judgment have occurred. There are a variety of subjective and objective causes that explain these differences.

On the subjective level we find different degrees of knowledge of the natural law in different societies, some more perfect, others more rudimentary. We cannot ignore the blinding consequences of vice and passions run amok in individual lives. It's a fact that lack of self-control can impede our judgment on moral questions. Different systems of education and the varying degrees of permissiveness in different societies contribute to this diversity of moral judgment, as well.

Over time the positive law in a society can come to conform more closely to the natural law. For example, slavery was once a common practice, with the masters enjoying an absolute authority over their "property." Gradually laws regarding the treatment of slaves were established, and eventually slavery was abolished. Today it is almost universally considered wrong because our understanding of human rights is better than in the past. This development shouldn't strike us as odd. Natural law, just like any other type of law, must be applied to particular cases. As we see its application to more and different situations, we see the natural law more fully; the natural law itself hasn't changed.

Social circumstances or customs do not decide what is right and wrong. It is universally true that one should do good and avoid evil. Progress in understanding what is good and what is evil is our progress in comprehending the natural law. According to the measure in which this knowledge advances in history, so too does man's responsibility to observe and follow the increasing exigencies of natural law.

All the human beings acknowledge some kind of morality; that is, they feel towards certain proposed actions the experiences expressed by the words "I ought" or "I ought not." These experiences . . . cannot be logically deduced from the environment and physical experience of the man who undergoes them. You can shuffle "I am forced" and "I shall be advised" and "I dare not" as long as you please without getting out of them the slightest hint of ought and ought not. . . . Attempts to resolve the moral experience into something else always presuppose the very thing they are trying to explain.

The Problem of Pain, C.S. Lewis

FALLACY #16:

I know he shouldn't do that, but he's a good guy.

Even though we are accustomed to call people by name of their actions (painters paint, bakers bake, and plumbers plumb), there is a growing tendency not to follow this logic when discussing morality. While we don't hesitate to think well of ourselves after doing a good deed, we're afraid to accept that our bad actions really do make us bad people.

RESPONSE TO THE FALLACY:

His actions are what make him good or bad. If his actions are bad, he's a bad guy.

We all share some fundamental goodness just for being here. It's kind of like the consolation prize they give away on game shows to the people who didn't win the new car or extravagant cruise complete with a box of "Rice-a-Roni." As we said in Chapter 5, being is a good that all things have. But we shouldn't content ourselves with just a basic level of goodness. If being is good, being good is even better.

Be all that you can be (or become all that you are)

We can say that while a person is, he is also becoming. What I mean is that we define ourselves by our acts. If a tree begins life growing straight, it will be a strong tree, but if a tree is crooked from early on, chances are it will always be bent and weak. Likewise, the person is the center of his own acts and, at the same time, the end product of them. So our freedom implies not only a decision about a particular act but also an integral decision about ourselves as a whole.

When we were young we used to start lots of conversations with, "When I grow up, I'm gonna . . ." In our moral acts we are making ourselves in the here and now what we will be when we are older. Through our actions for good or evil, we direct our lives toward good or evil, truth or falsity. Of course not all of our choices carry the same weight. We do make some general life-shaping choices that set the tone for our entire moral life and that serve as the guides and bound-aries for our actions. These choices can be considered as shaping a fundamental option for our lives.

The fundamental option is the choice by which every man decides, explicitly or implicitly, what global sense to give to his life, what type of man he wants to make of himself. It is a profound, free choice that orients and directs his existence. It becomes the most important nucleus of the human person because it is a choice about his own existence and the reality that surrounds him. But making one big decision about your fundamental option is not enough.

An option that should determine my options

In the last chapter we mentioned that man lives on a practical level and not on a theoretical level. That is, man fulfills himself or destroys himself in concrete instances, not in his theories or general plans or good intentions. By our free moral actions an authentic fundamental option for our lives is ratified, modified, or even wholly revised. Note carefully: We are free persons and our authentic fundamental option, freely chosen, can likewise be freely rejected. The fundamental option is not a determinant option, for it is the fruit of a free choice and we can always opt against it. We can nevertheless say that the authentic fundamental option is a dominant option; the mature person tends to judge his individual acts by his authentic fundamental option. The mature person lives his authentic fundamental option coherently and consistently, and it wields a progressively stronger influence over his particular choices as he progresses through life, confirming his initial decision in his individual acts. Even one conscious decision against the natural law will vitiate an authentic fundamental option for the good. Therefore, you need more than an authentic fundamental option, you need a sustained authentic fundamental option.

Imagine that as a child I decided to become a doctor because I wanted to relieve people's suffering. I studied but never practiced medicine and instead became a tattoo artist. Regardless of my original good intention and academic degree, I'm more of a tattoo artist than a doctor. Why? Because my daily actions have made me a better tattoo artist than a doctor. Similarly, if as an altar boy I decided that I wanted to be a great saint when I grew up and read all sorts of lives of the saints but in my daily life robbed the Sunday collection and burnt down orphanages as a hobby (or even just on one occasion), I would hardly be able to consider myself saintly, regardless of my good youthful intentions. My being, while being the foundation of my acts, is also, in a certain sense, the product of my acts.

Following this same logic, consider the example of a parent. A person who wants to be a good parent but ignores some of the many responsibilities of parenthood will not be considered a good parent. This may sound like a harsh or uncompassionate judgment on the parent, but in our global decisions about life we find that there are a lot more "don'ts" than "do's." That is, when we have taken upon ourselves a certain legitimate lifestyle, we sacrifice other possibilities. The mature person recognizes that he may not opt for things contrary to his choice and remain consistent with himself. A husband who has chosen one bride has rejected 2.5 billion others in the same act. Our fundamental option works the same way.

Repetition of virtue brings habit brings happiness

We can say, then, that man truly defines himself by exercising his particular and specific choices, in which he conforms himself to natural law and authentically fulfills his nature. Our judgments about morality must take into consideration whether or not the deliberate choice of a specific kind of behavior is in harmony with man's nature and his call to fulfill himself.

Our fulfillment is at stake in our every moral decision. We perfect ourselves through the option for the good, or we put our humanity (as well as our eternal friendship with God) in jeopardy. With every freely committed act against the good we not only offend the natural law, we also offend the Lawgiver. So, too, for every instance in which we fulfill the natural law, we fulfill ourselves as well and become what we are and what we are meant to be. This relationship between man as he is and as what he is becoming is the connection between being human and becoming perfect. And our happiness depends upon it.

FALLACY #17:

If it feels good, do it.

Man has a tendency to satisfy his appetites. Taking this as life-goal rather than a condition of life, the philosophical system called **hedonism** claims that man finds happiness only in sensual pleasure. The disciples of this school maintain that when pleasure doesn't bring happiness, at least it brings escape. The disproportionately high suicide rates in the most hedonistic of cultures suggest the question: Is it life's apparent lack of meaning that gives rise to the pursuit of sensual satisfaction, or does hedonism itself cause a certain desperation and emptiness? Whichever the case, pleasure-seeking and existential pain always seem to go together.

RESPONSE TO THE FALLACY:
Not everything that feels good is good for you. Not everything that is good for you feels good.

While most people recognize their own weakness in this area, and some are willing to admit their faults, most of them have enough self-respect not to champion pleasure as if it were an end in itself. Yet the epoch of "free love" almost turned all that around. "We have to liberate ourselves from imposed inhibitions"; "The Establishment and its Puritan traditions have enslaved us long enough—break those chains, be natural, be free!" I grew up hearing these robot-like chants but never quite climbed onto that bandwagon. At the time I couldn't discuss the meanings of the terms of the day—"nature," "freedom," "rights," and so forth—with much intelligence. More than any philosophical argument, it was seeing those terms used to legitimize practices from the innocuous to the unfathomable that caused me to question their real meaning.

I remember the day in high school when an acquaintance of mine told me he was more "free" since letting his long, red hair become an Afro so it could be more "natural." Somewhat perplexed at how one "lets" long straight hair become curly, I asked him his secret. "Easy, I go to the stylist and he curls it for me." Oh.

For the moment we'll stick to our definitions of freedom and nature.

Virtual reality or virtuous reality?

Equating feeling good with goodness is widespread. Pleasure is good and pain is evil. This error rests on a confusion between sensible good and evil and intelligible good and evil: Whatever feels good must be good, whatever feels bad couldn't possibly be good for me. Today more and more people seem to be absorbed into this void of virtual reality, and the consequences of this hedonism are tragic.

Shortly after Winston Churchill's election to the office of Prime Minister, as Britain was on the brink of certain war, he awoke one morning from pleasant dreams of a land with no conflict. Understanding the responsibilities that lay upon his shoulders in such a difficult time, his aides apparently "felt his pain" and murmured something about its being a pity to have to wake up to such nightmarish world. Churchill rejected their kind words saying, "I prefer the ugly truth to sweet untruths."

Suppose we were able to produce a virtual-reality machine that was all-encompassing, one in which you would never take off the helmet. You would be guaranteed the lifelong satisfaction of your every sensory desire, as long as you never peeked outside of the mask to see the real world. Would you go for it? Realizing that you would be detached from all human relationships and limited in your possibilities of self-development, you would most likely respond with a curt, "Thanks, but no thanks." Living inside a virtual-reality machine would exclude us from our loved ones, from society, and even, in a certain sense, from our very selves. Sort of like those people who wear walkmans (or is it walkmen?) and almost get run over because they're oblivious to the traffic around them. Hedonism, the self-absorbing practice of pleasure-seeking, truncates our spiritual and moral growth.

On the other hand, having made a choice for reality, one enjoys the many perks that come with it—the company of others, the ability to judge correctly and admire the virtue found in one's friends and family members. Human relationships are important for human growth, maturity, and happiness.

Hedonism or heroism?

I read an article in a national German newspaper the other day, reporting a rape at midday in a busy subway in downtown Munich. It reminded me of a similar episode on a crowded New York street in 1964, in which a woman was repeatedly stabbed. The onlookers listened and watched from their apartments until the victim died and the attacker escaped unopposed. No one did anything to stop the killing. Yet if someone had reacted positively and attempted to save the woman, he would have been hailed a hero. Why? Because he would have known how to see beyond his own repugnance for pain and to seek to do good for someone else at an unknown cost to his own person.

One might be tempted to respond "Yeah, but no one is obliged to help. It's too risky." Following that line of thought, we would have no cause to honor the would-be hero who intervened. He would be a deluded idealist. The tragedy of the slain woman is only increased by the bystanders' passivity. Hedonism is like that. It's too caught up in itself to consider someone else's needs.

Avoiding the other extreme, no one claims that everything painful is good and heroic and everything that feels good is bad. It seems that the level of physical sensitivity is too shallow a category with which to understand all reality. As spiritual and corporal beings, we should be able to recognize both physical and spiritual goods. Most things that feel good—health, cleanliness, friendship, and so forth—are in fact good. The problems arise when our criteria for good never transcend the sensory. The good in things that attracts us has its foundation in being, as we have seen. This fact is most obvious in persons: the exterior beauty of some persons can attract attention, but much stronger is the attraction of a virtuous person.

If the possession of goodness makes us happy, then we must ask ourselves whether things that cause happiness are necessarily good. Is the presence of happiness a certain indicator of goodness? Further, is there a scale of happiness? That is, are some of the many things that cause happiness of more value than others?

We know from experience that the person who acts only to satisfy himself receives little respect from those around him. He seems to degrade himself in his search for the "easiest way at any cost." The mature man, on the other hand, who suffers for what is just and right, immediately earns our respect. But this would make no sense if sense pleasure were the thermometer of good.

Pleasure or happiness?

We begin to see a distinction here. There seems to be a difference between pleasure and happiness. Whereas pleasure implies a provisional state, something grasped and soon to escape, happiness is more intimate and full. Happiness means a certain stability that resides on a more profound level than just the exterior senses. Happiness speaks of the harmony of the entire person. So that hedonism, while it may achieve certain goods, falls short. Living as hedonists we take a few small steps toward happiness, but never seem to grasp it in its entirety; we finally end up frustrated and empty.

The question in every instance is whether this or that action—even if it is disagreeable or painful—is going to contribute to my self-realization as a human person, the fulfillment of my human nature in accordance with the natural law. If we have a human nature, it permits us to choose perfection and fulfillment as a person. In that sense we can say that our human nature is not a confinement or a straitjacket, but an opportunity, a vocation, a project that is proposed to us and which we are free to accept or reject. Of course, we are always free to choose to live on a level inferior to our human vocation, but the great paradox is that this free choice frustrates our true objective and diminishes our human freedom.

It's your move

In order to decide what it is we want in life, what we recognize as our ultimate goal, it helps to consider on what level we find the things we consider goods. Are they aspects of persons or realities apart from persons? Are they congruous with my authentic fundamental option in life? Do they bring me lasting happiness, or just momentary satisfaction?

Our individual actions confirm, redirect, or revoke our fundamental option. Our fundamental option is constantly being brought into play through our conscious and free decisions. Those things we recognize as goods, those things to which we dedicate our lives (or even aspects of our life) by way of individual acts and not in a generic unspecified way, must be judged according to their conformity with the dignity and vocation we enjoy as human persons.

You gotta fight for your right to party.
Beastie Boys, 1986

FALLACY #18:

. . . Yeah, but it's my right!

I remember a discussion I had with another college student about abortion. He said parents should be able to take the lives of their unborn child, and I argued that nobody has this authority. I tried to base my arguments on reason alone, rather than on theological grounds. My opponent, on the other hand, apparently a minimalist debater, defended the taking of innocent life with one sentence: "Yeah, but it's my right."

Eventually he conceded that there was no doubt that the being in the womb of the mother was a living human person, that this person was innocent, and that man has no absolute authority over life. Thinking we had made some progress, I was nonplussed when he countered with, "Yeah, but it's still my right." We then discussed the possibility that positive laws do not always reflect natural law. I was convinced he understood the concepts. He nodded thoughtfully in assent and seemed to be on the brink of formulating a new sentence when suddenly he responded with a surprise tactic: "Yeah, but it's my right." I say "surprise" because I had thought, at least for a few minutes there, that we were actually communicating and were ready to embark upon an adventure in truth. No go. As a last effort I was tempted to ask him if knew what a "right" was, but fearing an answer such as "what I got" or "what's mine" or something to that effect, I left it at that.

RESPONSE TO THE FALLACY:
Define "rights," please.

I respond with "Define rights, please," not as a quick one-liner, but as a starting point. If we do not understand the meaning of words or the why of ethical principles, what we say and do will be little more than blurry half-truths. And half-truths are not true at all.

There is always the possibility that the person with whom we speak is incapable of getting beyond ideology. But if we can agree upon the meanings of words and use them consistently, we can make real advances.

The term "rights" is used to justify everything from the taking of unborn human life to getting drunk, as in that little gem of a song "You Gotta Fight for Your Right to Party." Rights also protect citizens and uphold the dignity of persons. So what are these things that protect some human beings, and at the same time can be the death sentence for others? What is a right? Define it, please.

Whose right?

First, let's see what **rights** are not, shall we?

Rights do not give me the absolute freedom to satisfy my desires regardless of the nature of these desires. Repeating over and over, "Yeah, but it's my right" doesn't mean anything unless we first understand the nature of the human person and the nature of the act which is said to be guaranteed by the right. If a right is whatever I want it to be, then who decides between conflicting "rights"? For example, if I claim that children have the right to life, and further, that I have the right to do everything in my power to save a baby's life, and another person claims the right to kill the child, whose right is right? Who intervenes to ensure that justice is done, and on what authority?

If we say that the judges or the government are the ultimate mediators of rights, then we have no right to condemn the officers of Nazi concentration camps, who faithfully obeyed their government and judiciary system.

In all the obscurity and contradictions of this discourse, one element has reappeared over and over again. This clue just may direct us to the answer: Everything we have said up until now has dealt with human interaction. In other words, an individual's rights do not exist except in relation to another person. Keep that in mind.

Who's right?

Another clue is that each defender of rights recognizes that what he deems a right is also a means towards a good. If goods are ends for persons, and man can make a moral claim upon those ends ("Yeah, but it's my right" would be one way of putting that claim), then perhaps we could say that rights are founded upon the objective fact of man's nature and end. Rights are derived from who man is and from man's natural end.

If a right is directly related to who man is and to man's natural end, then man should claim his rights. As a free and rational being, he has a moral responsibility to choose those means that will truly fulfill him and, choosing them, he should have access to them. Men have a right to do what is correct for them to do, and having been born with human nature, which is ordered toward certain natural ends, can make a claim on what we call "natural rights."

Rights from the start

Obviously, the most fundamental natural right is the right to life. Without it, there would be no other rights at all. In other words, to claim the right to kill the unborn is to absolutely deny the existence of all rights—a contradiction in terms. All other natural rights stem from this first natural right to life. We can logically deduce man's other rights from his nature as well. Man is a rational, spiritual being. Thus he has a right to freedom of conscience, freedom to worship God—in short, to everything that will contribute to his reaching his ultimate spiritual end. But man is not only spirit, as we have seen. The human person, as a physical being, has a right to shelter, clothing, food, medical treatment, employment, private ownership of property, and everything else that is necessary for him to survive and live a natural and fully human life. Notice that these rights are objective goods that correspond to man's nature; they are not arbitrary claims.

In other words, if we are free and are capable of recognizing what it is that will fulfill our nature, then we have a certain responsibility to use our freedom for this purpose. This means we have a certain responsibility to do good to ourselves according to the intention of our nature's Author.

All of this may sound obvious, but we are still missing the other element of what a right is. Who provides the things people have rights to? Rights have to do with human relationships just as much as they have to do with the dignity and worth of the individual, for without human interaction there would be no rights. If a child has a right to life, his parents have the duty to see that the child is born and well cared for. If that child also has rights to education, shelter, worship, nutrition, and clothing, then someone has to provide these things. Take the example of the right to education: the parents have the ultimate duty of providing for the fulfillment of their children's right to education, but this is a shared duty. The state also has the duty to make education available to the family. The pattern here is the relationship of rights with duties. A's rights correspond to B's duties towards A.

Rights and justice

The complexity begins when we begin to mix types of rights. Just as natural rights have their foundation in natural law, it makes sense that positive rights should spring from positive law. Natural rights have more weight than positive rights, just as positive law should never undercut natural law. In instances of conflict, natural rights always take precedence. No one is obliged to obey a positive law that contradicts the natural law. We need look no further than the Nazi concentration camps to see this principle exemplified. Positive law obliged men to do inhumane things to human persons, but no one had a right to contradict the natural law in order to fulfill the positive law. No rights for such behavior means no duties to fulfill such positive law. But in cases in which the positive law does not contradict natural law in any way, one has a duty to follow the positive law.

Notice the pattern in this example: My nature does not require that I go water skiing; therefore, I do not have a natural right to go water skiing. Nonetheless, regardless of my natural talent (or lack of talent) for water skiing, there is no contradiction of any higher law here, and if I pay for a pair of water skis, the store has a duty to provide me with them; if I pay the necessary fees, the boat owner has a duty to drag me through the water at top speed. In other words, I can claim a positive right (not a natural right) to water ski. This is a mere exchange of goods—money for a legitimate pleasure. If the sought-after service or product were in conflict with natural law, then there would be no positive right to enjoy it, and no duty on anybody's part to provide it.

The first right

In the case of abortion, "Yeah but it's my right" does not automatically convince. For that matter, neither does "No, it's not your right." We could go on indefinitely gainsaying each other, but the basic problem is that rights, as we have seen, are not basic. We have to use reason to get to them. First we look at moral principles, at who man is and what is proper for man according to the natural law. Then, and only then, can we claim rights of any kind. Rights, as we have seen, are not a moral principle but a moral conclusion. If the foundation of rights is the natural law, and to live is what is most natural for a person, then the most fundamental right is the right to life. All other rights hinge on the fact of existing life. A corpse has no rights, but all human life does. To deny the right to life is to deny all subsequent rights. To appeal to the authority of the Supreme Court's decision is to call into question the condemnations of the Nazi and Stalinist regimes, which also appealed to positive law as the highest law.

"Yeah, but it's my right . . ."

I know nah-zing!
Sergeant Schultz, *Stalag 13*

FALLACY #19:

I vas just followink orders.

At the end of the Second World War many of the men who had committed atrocities justified their actions on the grounds of obedience to their superiors. Nonetheless, the majority of them were found guilty. If they were guilty for following immoral orders, then logically they should have followed a higher law than the positive law. The judges at Nuremberg declared that knowing how to act in diverse circumstances requires a well-formed conscience.

RESPONSE TO THE FALLACY:
Whose orders?

Thank goodness for conscience. Our whole discussion of the natural law would be useless without it. The role of the conscience is to apply the moral law to concrete situations. As we have mentioned previously, man has a profound awareness of himself, his thoughts, and his acts. This awareness is the conscience which, in the role of teacher, counsels a man before he acts, categorizing his acts in advance: "This is good, do it," or "This is bad, better not." Each man is free to follow or reject the commands of his conscience. But the conscience doesn't quit there. It also serves as a witness while a man is acting, testifying to the morality or immorality of each act. Thus man is aware not only of his acts but of their moral value as well. After the act, the conscience works as a judge, handing down approval or condemnation of the act committed.

Faulty packaging, or misused freedom?

A question immediately arises. If we come equipped with a conscience that tells us what is right and wrong, why do we still sometimes do evil? There are some cases in which the requirements of right reason perhaps are not so clear, resulting in doubt, confusion, or even ignorance. In fact, most of our evil choices are accompanied by a certain degree of obscurity, since we only choose what appears to have value. Obviously, in these cases we are judging in the here and now, while we often feel repentance in hindsight. Nonetheless, these evil choices are choices freely made. They have our free will for their foundation, but we have allowed a depraved appetite to influence us in these choices. When making an evil choice, we permit our reason to be dominated by the irrational, but all the while we know deep down that our choice is wrong. When we act in opposition to our conscience, we do evil. I know that I shouldn't cheat on exams. It goes against my reason. This is clear and simple. Yet simultaneously I recognize that there might be some benefits for me if I do. So I allow the desire for a higher grade to overcome my knowledge that it's more reasonable to do my own exam and hope for the best. If I choose to entertain this temptation and fall into it, my will has made the decision to call an unworthy act reasonable and blind my reason in the process. The evil of this blindness is that it is freely accepted, generated by my own decision, and often results in permanent distortion of my perception of what is rational.

It's easy to assent to these first principles: "Do good; avoid evil." And everyone wants to enjoy the benefits of a serene and upright conscience. The problems arise when we must decide for ourselves how to apply those principles to individual acts surrounded by circumstances that cloud our vision. In other words, we may not objectively be choosing the good, but subjectively we see nothing wrong with our behavior. Or perhaps we lack certainty in our acting: a doubtful conscience can hesitate between "yes" and "no" before the act.

For your information and formation

It is clear that we must always obey our conscience in order to remain blameless. But what about the cases in which our conscience is objectively mistaken? We must remember that the conscience is quite fallible. If someone suspects that his conscience may be in error and he knows that some investigation would illumine his judgment, he is obligated to find out what is correct. This done, it's all systems go. But, should he become aware of the availability of information he needs to inform his conscience and yet do nothing to obtain that information, his action is bad. He has what is called vincible error and is culpable (though the culpability may be somewhat mitigated by various circumstances). We always have a duty to form and inform our consciences. On the other hand, if someone proceeds believing he is doing good without the least suspicion of his error, or if he doesn't realize the relevance of his ignorance to his act, his error is invincible. Finally, there are those who blatantly and knowingly misuse their freedom. This is culpable error.

Note that vincible error isn't necessarily culpable, except to the extent that someone, suspecting his error, continues in it. In this manner the will can become evil, as a result of evil choices. On the other hand, someone who hasn't an inkling of the evil of his choice does not become evil by obeying his conscience. In fact, he is even obliged to obey his erroneous conscience in order to avoid any taint of guilt. But key to his blamelessness is the condition of involuntary and invincible error. The invincibly ignorant person does not escape the demands of conscience, even if it is an erroneous one. If what is wrong appears to him to be morally correct, he must opt for it; but he should always be seeking to further inform his conscience so as to act with rectitude.

Amongst the culpably ignorant we find several categories. There are those who choose not to know the moral value of a certain act because they fear this knowledge would prohibit them from committing the act with a semblance of peace of mind. Their willful ignorance not only adds to the guilt of the act. This interior division could lead to psychological problems in the individual.

There are also those who, out of negligence of duty, do not possess the appropriate information and act erroneously. Think of someone who hasn't learned the rules of the road and because of his lack of knowledge disobeys the signs and crashes into another car. Telling the judge that he didn't read that particular chapter before he tested for his driver's license is not going to help him in court.

Finally, there are those who possess knowledge of the evil nature of an act—running somebody over, for example—and nonetheless put themselves in the condition to bring it about: drunk driving. They don't wish to kill people, and they know that drinking and driving can result in death. But because of impeded judgment, they choose to drive. The first error was in getting drunk; all the rest is fruit of this culpable error.

Like many of the most important things in life, living according to one's conscience is simple. Simple, that is, in the sense of uncomplicated. Yet we often find it difficult to stay on track. The secret to fidelity to the conscience is to inform it (consulting the natural law and its particular applications) and to form it (practicing obedience to the conscience in order to develop good habits). Informing and forming our consciences often requires tremendous presence of mind and lots of courage. But in spite of all the pressures to give in to weakness and betray the conscience, there is no comparison to the peace one experiences after having overcome temptation and remained faithful to one's solidly formed principles.

If God does not exist, everything is permitted.
Jean-Paul Sartre, paraphrasing Fyodor Dostoyevsky

FALLACY #20:

Ethics are a personal matter, so what I do is my own business!

This is a tempting attitude and quite prevalent in certain circles of the First World. Newspapers, books, and college professors preaching this dogma abound, and throngs of disciples reverently bend the knee in obeisance to it. Other variations on this same theme are "I don't care what you do as long as you don't hurt anybody" and the really profound "whatever floats your boat, Dude. . . ."

But this lifestyle choice, also known as radical individualism, is made at great expense.

RESPONSE TO THE FALLACY:
You're right; ethics is an extremely personal matter that involves other persons, so what you do is their business too.

The fundamental difficulty here is the idea that **ethics** only has to do with one's immediate dealings with other people. Not quite.

We have already proven that God exists and that God, by nature, must be all-knowing. No matter where we hide, or how dark it may be, or how confused our thoughts are, the all-knowing God sees and knows them. So we can say that our every act is an interpersonal act, for we are always acting before God—whether we like it or not, whether we are aware of Him or not. If we deny God's existence, then any discussion of ethics is absurd. If God does not exist, we have no moral norm to follow, because nobody is above man to mandate how man ought to behave.

To answer, "There is no God, but there is human nature, and that is our guide," does not change this result. Human nature without God does not convince me to behave. Why should I? What's in it for me? If there is a human nature and no God, what are the consequences of rebelling against my nature and just doing whatever I want, even if it does harm somebody else? In this case, the only "evil" would be getting caught and punished; my actions, in and of themselves, would be morally indifferent.

Nonetheless, let's deal with the question at hand from a purely pragmatic (and horizontalist) approach, without making reference to God (and our vertical relationship to him).

No man is an island (or a peninsula, or a continent, or . . .)

Although ethics is not limited to human relationships, our interactions with each other provide the clearest examples when we're discussing ethics. Think about Chapter 4 on the human soul, in which we proved that man is spirit from his ability to think about his own thoughts and reflect on his own reflections. (By the way, that's what you call a *reditio completa* in Latin—in case you were wondering.) Society presents man with a similar opportunity. Through our interactions with other human beings we can overcome temptations to individualism and also find out lots of things about ourselves. How many times have we surprised ourselves by lending a hand to someone we don't really care for, or done some other spontaneous act of charity, which, if we had calculated the human cost, we most likely never would have done? How many times have we discovered our own limitations through our impatience or through our own harsh words? Relationships with others can tell us more about ourselves than about others because through them we understand who we are and discover our capabilities and weaknesses. Only through society and participation in human relationships can this occur.

Since human development requires human interaction, we can conclude that man is social by nature rather than by choice. Think about it. Every aspect of our lives is intertwined with the lives of others: your birth was not your own choice, and even your conception depended on the cooperation of other human beings. You are capable of speaking, which means you were pre-packaged with all the latest technology you need to tell the doctor what's ailing you, to politely take a pass on Aunt Grace's candied oysters at Christmas dinner, or to propose marriage. And people will understand you. Isn't that amazing? You learned how to speak from others, and can teach others in turn. Everything about our human lives is touched by human relationships and sociability in some way. You are equipped to interact with other persons because you were made to interact with them. You were made for society, and, better still, society was made for you.

Since our thoughts and actions define who we are and thus determine how we will act in the future, they affect other people. Since man is meant to live amongst others, it is a little difficult to hold that human action is purely a private affair.

Our very existence depends upon others, and other people depend upon us. Sociability is no accident or whimsical human choice. And that you should be sociable implies no infringement on your freedom.

In fact, the societal nature of man is not just a condition of our lives but a way to true freedom. Only in human relationships do we discover who we are and enjoy the opportunity to develop ourselves and become what we should be. This participation in society is a condition of our freedom in that it excludes treating others as objects or being treated as an object.

Someone might interject here and say, "That's fine. But I can still do whatever I want, as long as I don't hurt anyone else. My dwelling on nasty thoughts about other people, for example, doesn't harm them."

Thankfully, other people cannot read our thoughts. But our thoughts still have consequences. You can say your habitual nasty thoughts about someone else are purely your private affair and that this habit has no societal effect. Perhaps not immediately. But this sad little **habit** certainly won't help you to become a happier person. Ultimately, your way of thinking is going to surface in your relationships with other people. Your habits of thought are going to influence how you act toward the person you're having these nasty thoughts about. How we act—even in the privacy of our own minds—defines who we are and subsequently does enter into the realm of our dealings with others.

On the other hand, if you participate in society without treating others as objects or as personal belongings, then your scope action is indeed limited by the realization that what you do is somebody else's business. When children live by this code, we say they have "good manners." When adults live this way, we say they are mature.

Through his dealings with others in society, man becomes aware of his own value, discovers his true self, and sees more clearly how to direct his personal development. Similar to the *reditio completa* in which the intellect reflects upon itself is the human interaction in which man discovers himself through reflection on his interaction with another. Thus we can say that the authentic "I" is known only through the encounter with a "You."

Like son, like father

Think of the experience of an infant. He isn't sure about too much. His everyday sights and sounds get a bit fuzzy and blend into a collage of sense stimulation. When visitors stick their uninvited heads into his crib and begin to make faces and strange sounds, he doesn't know exactly what is going on, but most likely he doesn't think things like that improve the quality of his life by any measurable degree. He could do without it.

But it's different when Mom picks him up. He recognizes the loving smile, the familiar and maternal voice. He literally doesn't have words to describe his experience. Nonetheless, his whole being registers "this is good." What is good? The face of his mother, obviously. Her voice, too. But there's more to it than that. The whole thing is good. In this early experience of utter goodness the infant discovers, indirectly, that he is good. There is an experience of goodness that is only possible through human interaction. Although his conclusion is not verbalized, the infant has an experience of his own value—a conclusion that would have been impossible without another person.

Appreciating others and realizing ourselves through interactions with them does not stop when we stop being infants. These experiences pervade every aspect of human life. Human beings mature through friendships and are fulfilled in that most profound of human interactions: matrimonial love. Notice the inherent contradiction between individualistic ethics and the almost universal call to matrimony and family life. A young man and woman who fall in love find that their lives are completely altered. The mundane things of life are suddenly important if they are somehow connected to the beloved. The lover is capable of coming out of himself and making sacrifices in order to be with his beloved or please her. He is happy because the other person has come into his life. The man discovers that not only is life good but it has become better because of her. As a result of this human relationship, he discovers that his life, his very self, is good. By affirming the beloved, the lover indirectly affirms himself and discovers that what he does, even if it is secret and unseen, has consequences and value and should be worthy of his beloved. In a certain way, we can say that through human love you discover yourself anew, give yourself to the beloved, and receive yourself once again in a new form.

What price radical individualism?

Love is truly the gift of self. So when a man truly loves a woman, he must ask himself if his thoughts, words and works (in short, the self he is offering to her) are worthy of his beloved. After all, when a man loves a woman, he gives all that he is to her. The more he loves, the more he wants to give his beloved something of value. The only way to increase the value of his gift is to be a better man. Love is an exchange not of promises but of persons. When the lover says, "I'm all yours"—not in superficial way, but in a way that commits him totally—that is **love**.

Man derives his greatest happiness from loving and being loved. Love is total self-giving, and the nature of that gift of self includes all that one does and thinks. So there really is no totally private ethic. And it's a good thing. Consider the logical consequences, if radical individualism were true. We could say that ethics were a purely private affair, but only if we were willing to give up true love.

. . . Till the one day when the lady met this fellow...
Brady Bunch theme song, 1970s

FALLACY #21:

It doesn't matter if two consenting adults are married or not; what counts is their sincerity.

Running a bit late (as usual) I was surprised to find that there was still one empty seat left on the morning train from a small Bavarian town to Cologne. I sat down next to a woman about 50 years old. As the train picked up a bit of momentum, so did our conversation—only to be interrupted when a young priest walked by. The woman became irate. "Celibacy," she claimed, "is a fraud; no one can live it." I kind of chuckled at this turn of events. At one moment we had been discussing German politics in a light manner. In the next moment her entire demeanor changed; she looked ready to start a crusade against purity. But my surprise turned to sorrow for her as she went on to finish her thesis on why self-control was not normal, healthy, or possible. I asked her how many men she had lived with. She burst out crying and told me that on that very morning she had collected her things and was moving up North to begin her life again after number eight "just didn't work out." She couldn't stop crying.

RESPONSE TO THE FALLACY:
Then why has every culture in every age recognized human love as best expressed (and safeguarded) within the institution of marriage?

In these chapters dedicated to matrimony, I do not intend to address particular or extreme cases. What interests us here are the basic principles—the foundations of the institution of matrimony, as well its characteristics.

There really is a difference between you and a halibut

Some argue that since the sexual appetite is natural, it ought not to be confined to marriage. People should be allowed to express themselves sexually, as they see fit. Taking this line of thought to its logical consequences gets us to a rather pessimistic view of the human person. To give our urges primacy is to put human dignity on a level with the dignity of the animals, which can only follow instinct. While animals and men share the instinctual desire for nutrition and procreation, there are substantial differences between animal and human nature. Man, as a composite of body and soul—flesh and bone mixed with intellect and will—is capable of enjoying the pleasures of eating and procreating more than an animal ever could. On the other hand, as a corporal and spiritual person, he can sublimate the instincts that the animals follow blindly. In other words, there is no real comparison between animals and human person. It's not a question of apples and oranges; it's more like the difference between you and a halibut.

Even man's instincts differ from the animals' instincts. We have an instinctual sense of shame or modesty that the animals do not share. Your pet dog, for example, does lots of things in full view that you wouldn't dream of doing at even the most informal of parties.

Of course, it's possible to ignore the dictates of reason and the messages you receives from your conscience and live on the merely sensory-instinctual level. But you're still not living like a halibut. Unlike a fish, you're living like an animal because you choose to—and you could choose to live by virtue instead. The halibut has no such choice.

Living a life limited to instinct or seeking only to please your latest physical urge is like having the latest computer equipment, only to use the computer as a door wedge. You are not fulfilled as a human person, the purely physical gratifications subside, and pleasure becomes pain. The human person was created for something much greater than mere sensuality. Man is thirsty for something that transcends "the thrill of the moment."

Love's natural and logical context: marriage

What are the most obvious ends of the conjugal act? If we are confined to the level of instinct, then the only answer is survival of the species. But we have already established that man is more than an animal; he is also spirit. Animals and man copulate in order to ensure the existence of the species, but man was made to do more than exist. Man can love. The conjugal act, then, is not only the natural means of bringing about new human life, it is also an expression of love and a means to renew and grow in love. This is another difference between us and the animals.

So if the two obvious ends of the conjugal act are new life and a renewal of love, we can say that we have found the natural foundations for **marriage**. We'll investigate these two characteristics of marriage in more depth in upcoming chapters, but first let's consider what is even prior to marriage—human love.

"I" is spelled with a "You"

Remember the role of the "You" in discovering the true "I." The development of the human person takes place in the context of interpersonal interaction. It is not enough for the infant to receive his eight essential vitamins. If the child doesn't experience human love, he suffers tremendously; often babies in these circumstances do not survive. Later in life adolescents and adults become capable of forming friendships. These can be founded on a common interest or ideal or just a great mixture of personalities. But the most profound human relationship is that of a man and woman in love. In this case it is not simply "You" and "I," but "We." Between the two lovers there is a mutual identity that alters each one's way of thinking and acting. Suddenly the beloved is the object of one's thoughts, sentiments, and plans. Love says: *I am all yours. Will you be all mine?* As we have seen, the difference between infatuation and authentic love is this attitude of total self-giving. There is an inherent weakness in the moment a lover declares his love, exposing his intentions to the mercy of the beloved, who may reject him. He takes a risk and puts himself at the mercy of the beloved's free reply. It has to be that way; if it were any other way it would not be love. The covenant of marriage, as a natural institution, is a form of shelter for the two lovers. It is the assurance of the seriousness of both, as well as the societal ratification of their relationship.

If this life-commitment is missing, then what the couple has is not real love. And if they engage in the procreative act out of mere infatuation or pleasure-seeking, their act goes against the dignity of the person. No one should be used as an object or as a means to an end outside of the person himself. To defend two persons' using one another just to satisfy their appetites—with the argument that each is making a free decision—falls short of reason. If we live in a way that casts reason aside in the name of pleasure, without any real commitment to lasting love, then maybe we're not so different from halibuts.

TV has embarked on a new era of candor, with all the lines emphatically drawn in. . . . Religious quirks, wife-swapping, child abuse, Lesbianism, venereal disease—all the old taboos will be toppling.

Time Magazine, 25 September 1972

FALLACY #22:

The traditional family structure is arbitrary. Actually there are many equally valid arrangements.

The last few decades have witnessed some surprising twists and turns. The question at hand in many places is whether or not men may legally marry men and whether women may marry women. At the root of the problem is a new anthropology. As we saw in Chapter 12, some are arguing that there are not just two sexes, but five genders. So homosexual "marriages" should receive all the recognition and benefits of heterosexual marriages.

Can we take "X," empty it of its original meaning, fill it with "Y," and then demand that others recognize it as an "X" entitled to all the benefits of "X"—with no other justification than we want it to be that way? The question is whether or not we are at liberty to take the nature of something essential to human existence and alter its definition simply by willing it to be something different.

Can we redefine the nature of things at the whims of pressure groups? Or by majority vote? (Not that the majority would, in fact, vote for homosexual marriage.)

May we delineate the boundaries of reality? On what authority? Who decides if our definitions of reality are valid or not? The state? On what authority can the state define or confine our definitions of reality?

Are the state and the law there to serve man or have we, somewhere along the way, gotten it backwards?

RESPONSE TO THE FALLACY:

Not really. Either it is a family or it's not. Definitions are dependent on reality, not on ideology.

A few chapters back we discussed the differences between man and woman in the context of diversity and complementarity. Human nature, as observed since man's first appearance on the planet, has exhibited diversity and complementarity. At the root of the misunderstanding of the sexes is a misunderstanding of who the human person is and how the human person fulfils himself. In this chapter we return to the same fundamental error, but focus on the role of the law in regulating human relationships.

What is marriage, anyway?

Is marriage the servant of the law and the political order—even of pressure groups and their lobbyists? Or is law at the service of the human person, and therefore, of marriage?

First of all, when we discuss the traditional kind of marriage, between a man and a woman, it's important to remember that we are speaking about a way of life experienced, accepted, and approved by man since before man could record his behavior. In other words, marriage is an integral part of the natural law and intimately connected to how man should realize himself. So maybe we should consider what we may be discarding or altering by acting rashly.

What is marriage? Looking at the empirical facts—how man has lived throughout history and how the vast majority of people live today—we can say that marriage is the permanent and exclusive union of persons of opposite sexes involved in an intimate covenant for the purpose of building a family together. This covenant is ratified by society through a contract.

Perhaps we should first distinguish between the nature of the institution of marriage, as described above, and a marriage in particular—the free decision of this man and this woman to form a small society composed of themselves and their children, confirmed with a legitimate contract. What makes the contract legitimate is the free decision of both the man and the woman and their willingness and preparedness to embark upon the life that is natural to a family: sexual relations, procreation, the rearing and educating of their children, life together in community. This is the nature of the **family**, and it corresponds to the nature of man. Thus the institution of marriage, proceeding as it does from human nature, is prior to any individual marriage, and it cannot be altered—either by any individual couple or by the state—to be something that it is not. Marriage is something prior to the state. So it is not the legal contract created by the state that makes the couple one, but the couple themselves, if they fulfill the requirements of nature.

Marriage's design or designer marriage?

If marriage is a primordial human reality flowing from man's nature, then, as the first human society, it should take precedence over all other social structures. The state, therefore, is obliged to promote the family and protect it from everything that may impede it from fulfilling its natural end.

The nature of things means how things are in reality, not how we want them to be because of some ideology. "Natural" as applied to the human person and the institutions of marriage and the family means that man was made a certain way: for sexual union with a member of the opposite sex within the context of a stable, exclusive, permanent bond freely chosen by both parties. Nature and instinct play their roles in marriage, but marriage cannot be reduced to the natural sexual instinct. On the one hand, marriage is not merely the fruit of human deliberation. Marriage was not invented by us; it arises from our natural impulses to provide for the good of the species and the individual, from the demands of our nature. On the other hand, we are not simply at the mercy of the blind forces of nature. Nature stimulates, but right reason and human love assent to that stimulation and guide our response to it. So there are actually two sides to the marriage-and-family coin: The nature of marriage and the nature of the family are discovered in man's nature, but each actual marriage is brought into being by the free consent of the husband and wife, which implies consent to the institution of marriage, with all of its pre-requisites and obligations. The desire of one of the spouses—or even the agreement of both of them—cannot alter what marriage and family really are.

"Homosexual marriage," therefore, doesn't fulfill the pre-requisites for marriage, beginning with the primary requirement for matrimonial love: two persons of opposite sexes. The fruitful mutual self-giving in heterosexual marriage, which strengthens the matrimonial bond between the two spouses and also brings about new life, is lacking in the "homosexual marriage." A homosexual relationship may involve a certain love for the other person, but that love can never be life-giving, and the relationship does not partake of the natural matrimonial bond, which is a union of naturally complementary persons.

In unfruitful love, there is little to keep the couple united. As a result, homosexual relationships lack stability. There's a notorious lack of exclusivity and permanence of relationships in the homosexual culture.

On the other hand, from true (heterosexual) marriage comes the family. Certain elements of the family transcend time and place: the conjugal union sanctioned by society, the duties of parents to raise and educate their children, stable community life amongst the family members. All of these are conditions for fulfillment of the individual person.

As one of the principal vehicles for the fulfillment of the person, and as the first cell of human society, marriage and family tell us a lot about who man is. Observing marriage and family life teaches us about realities of human nature and what it requires for preservation and fulfillment: complementarity between man and woman, aptitude to procreate and educate, and so forth. Certainly man is prior to the state. (How could you have a state without having people first? How could you have people without procreation?) Therefore the family, while enjoying the support of the state, doesn't require the state to exist or to be legitimate. The family, as a natural institution, is the first complete society upon which the greater society and the state are founded and remain dependent. The priority of the family is important to keep in mind, especially because the authority of the state (something posterior to human persons and marriage) is often invoked as a sort of divine umpire to decide the definition of marriage—and even of man himself: whether or not he should be allowed to come into existence, in what manner he may do this, and (at the end of his life) whether or not he is of value any longer. We have already opened the door to "disposable marriages" and now to "designer marriage," to "disposable children" and "designer children," to "disposable sick and elderly." All of this suddenly becomes acceptable if we just change the definitions of words and forget about the nature of things.

But the nature of things is precisely the question. May we change the meaning of a concept, even if that concept is *man*? Can we define what we are by legislation—or court decisions? If marriage and family are expressions of human nature, and their demands are to be subject to the law (not vice versa), then we had better prepare ourselves for the chaos that follows whenever human beings toy with the natural order. Do we want to accept reality and its demands and put the law at the service of marriage and family, or do we want to put marriage and family in servitude to the law?

Truth or consequences?

If we opt for the word game over reality, we had better prepare ourselves to live with the consequences. For example, just because we want it so, we could decide to transplant trees, but this time roots up and branches buried in the ground. It may not seem like a brilliant thing to do, but if we're in the business of rewriting the laws of nature, what is dumb, after all? Of course, the roots of a tree need the protection and nutrients that the soil provides, and the tree will die in short order. But no matter. Reality is what we say it is. We can even organize pressure groups to get judges and politicians to proclaim those withered, sterile trees to be just like normal, fruit-bearing trees. Because our freedom allows us to.

Or why not get a court of law to declare garbanzo beans to be Valencia oranges? Just imagine the money we could make by requiring customers to pay the price of an orange for a bean. After all, we're free to say what an orange really is. *But that wouldn't correspond to reality,* you say? *It's unbelievable*? Not really. Marriage and the family are being redefined in the name of the same freedom.

Yes, but we are not talking about fruits (no pun intended), we are talking about persons. Of course, and that makes it all the more serious.

If we believe that everyone should be encouraged to satisfy his every sexual desire—even have his favored form of sexual expression ratified by the state—why stop at homosexual marriages? And, come to think of it, why stop with liberating sexual impulses? Why not allow pyromaniacs and kleptomaniacs to fulfill their impulses, too, if they feel they were born that way?

Sexual impulses alone are no foundation for a family, nor is the human will divorced from reason. Until now, promiscuity has never been considered a value in any culture. The normal mutual attraction between a man and a woman and their physical complementarity speak of natural, fruitful sexuality and constitute the normal foundation for marriage and family. Homosexuality lacks these elements. Homosexuals are not physically compatible. Homosexual acts are not natural. And homosexual relationships certainly do not bring about new life.

The fact that the proposed new forms of marriage and family have suddenly come into existence, and that their legitimacy must be argued for without any precedent in human history, demonstrates that they are the constructs of a few and do not correspond to human nature. The vast majority of people have always lived in the context of the natural family and continue to do so. We are allowing a small but vociferous minority that insists upon making marriage something other than it is impose their ideology on us.

Perhaps the reason things have gone so far is that we have forgotten the right order of things. We are allowing law to define reality instead of remembering that law is the servant of man.

If a man were to give everything he owned for love, he would

count it as nothing.

Song of Songs 8:7

FALLACY #23:

Monogamy is an outdated social structure imposed on us by Judeo-Christian culture. (At least that's what I learned at college!)

In the nineteenth century, Marx and other Communists claimed that monogamy was just one phase in the development of the family, following on a long line of other arrangements. Monogamy in its turn would be followed by other developments. In the twentieth century the Nazi movement, armed with the latest "scientific" findings of the intellectual and cultural elite, claimed something similar—going so far as to set up controlled birthing programs amongst those believed to be of "Aryan" stock. One can easily find traces of this thinking today among people who define themselves not by race or social class but by "gender identification" or "sexual orientation." They believe that monogamy is a thing of the past and that mankind is on the verge of experiencing another development in matrimony and family life that will make monogamy and traditional male-female marriage a relic of the past, like a curio from someone else's garage sale.

Interestingly, all the opponents of traditional family structures are themselves results of the time-tested "mixed marriage," that is, the union of one man and one woman.

RESPONSE TO THE FALLACY:

Judeo-Christian culture also imposed hospitals, orphanages, and even the concept of the university on us. But that doesn't make them less valuable.

Exclusivity: a gift for two

Ever since Jacob's kids in the Book of Genesis, children of polygamous marriages have suffered from the tensions inherent in marriage without monogamy. Although harem-style polygamy is no longer so common, it's still a common occurrence for one man to have several wives—perhaps now more than ever. Rather than simultaneous polygamy, our society permits and promotes successive polygamy in the form of divorce and remarriage. Rather than delivering on its promise of total freedom for individuals, the successive polygamy made possible by easy divorce and remarriage—no less than simultaneous polygamy—devalues the human person.

Besides divorce and remarriage, there are two forms of multiple-spouse marriage that have been practiced on a small scale: **polygamy** (multiple wives) and **polyandry** (multiple husbands). (By the way, even in those countries where the civil law and religious law permit polygamy—Islamic countries, for example—few practice it. In fact,

less than 1% of the population think polygamy preferable to monogamy.) Polygamy presents us with a disturbing scenario in which the
woman is treated as a possession. In polygamous marriages women
suffer injustice and feel they must compete for attention, since the
husband always prefers one wife to the others. Polyandry may provide
the matriarch with a few more hunters and gatherers, but it creates
an injustice for the children in the form of an identity crises: they can
never be quite sure which of the fine gentlemen in their lives is really
Dad. At the core of both these deficient forms of family life is a misunderstanding of the nature of spousal love. And, as we've seen since
the explosion of divorce in the twentieth century, familial instability
is a self-perpetuating problem.

A stable union of one father and one mother gives the human person
a first and lasting pattern for personal development and points to the
infinite value of the human person as well. The truly (not temporar-
ily) monogamous marriage is, therefore, better for everyone. Children
want their parents to stay together, and the children of faithful parents
are more likely to succeed in monogamy than children of polygamous
parents. In other words, Mom, Dad, and the kids agree on this one.

Regardless of the divorce statistics, most brides and grooms want
their marriage to last. They recognize that among the fundamental
characteristics of their union, it is **exclusivity** that increases their love
for each other, as well as ensuring the completeness of their union.

Complete self-giving can only be understood (and practiced)
through exclusivity, which is opposed to mere possession of the other.
Exclusivity means you are all mine, but it also means I am all yours.
To decide for a spouse in this way, to declare your life will be totally
given to another in matrimonial union is to proclaim the singular
and unrepeatable value you find in your beloved—and such a proc-
lamation automatically excludes any other. This self-giving protects
matrimonial love from becoming possessiveness: without exclusivity,
self-giving gives way to selfish taking.

Many who have suffered through divorce recognize that "it would
have been better if it had worked out"—suggesting that stable and
exclusive matrimony is the preferable arrangement. When men or

women engage in marital infidelity, the fact that they try to keep their affairs secret implies that they at least recognize exclusivity as a value—a value worth pretending to, even if not worth really having.

Permanence: a gift from two

Obviously there are extreme cases. But in the U.S. more than 50% of marriages break up. Are those all extreme cases?

Why the hesitation to accept the commitment to marriage forever? Immaturity. Not being able to say I accept you as you are, with all that this commitment implies, is a definite sign that this love is not real—or, at least, that this love is not yet mature.

Matrimonial love doesn't mean *I will love you in good times, but when things get rough it's Adios*. True matrimonial love means *I love you, and therefore I accept you totally with all that this commitment implies, no matter what this commitment may bring*. Yes, matrimony is a risk and a total commitment. Therefore, it frightens the immature person. But it intrigues the true lover. This commitment is made, not in the certainty that either spouse is capable of fulfilling the requirements of marriage, but with the confidence that together they can.

The wedding bond is just that: a bond. Through this bond man and wife give themselves to each other, as opposed to loaning or pawning themselves. This offering of oneself to another, when done maturely and seriously, means that the lover will live entirely for the beloved. The experience of this kind of love, in which the beloved is the object of one's thoughts, desires, and life, transcends mere erotic love. The difference is best seen in the **permanence** of marriage. The stark and blunt words *I love you* imply total commitment. To add anything to these words—for example, *I love you a lot* or *You know, I love you, and I really mean that*—seems to cheapen them and call the lover's declaration into question.

A declaration of love is not a manifestation of infatuation, and it is much more than an expression of fondness or even friendship. It is a declaration of the value one sees in the beloved and of one's intention to commit oneself totally to the beloved. The words *I love you* and their fulfillment in the marriage bond create a union of two bodies and souls that is non-negotiable. This union means permanence. This radical self-giving cannot be repeated with another during the life of the promised spouse. Wedding vows are promises of love pronounced in public to ensure the seriousness of the gift of self because there may come a time when one of the spouses will have to rely on the force of the vow to stay faithful. Man is weak. And it is only prudent to safeguard something as solemn as matrimony from the ups and downs that man's weakness produces.

The very nature of the conjugal act requires the context of a stable and exclusive matrimonial union.

Stability is necessary

For the couple: Without stability, the sexual union is sensuality without responsibility. Man instinctively understands that promiscuous sexuality is unworthy of human dignity: hence our sense of modesty and shame. Shamelessness may be increasing today, but most of us still feel the force of the instinct to modesty—and it's a good thing!

For the children. Procreation without stability is harmful for the children, who need to be raised and educated by their parents over an extended period of time. The complementary contributions of the two very different parents are indispensable for the best education of the children.

The matrimonial bond is a reality that is fruitful for the spouses as they live it day by day—and also a permanent goal towards which they impel themselves and each other. The true lover knows through experience that the matrimonial bond transcends each individual spouse. Matrimony's fruitfulness goes far beyond the good of the couple: it brings about new life. The supreme gift of marriage is the children it produces.

Hear, nature, hear! Dear goddess, hear!
Suspend thy purpose, if thou didst intend
To make this creature fruitful.
Into her womb convey sterility,
Dry up in her the organs of increase....
King Lear, William Shakespeare

FALLACY #24:

No one's going to tell me how many children I'm going to have!

Often people claim the rights to do or to not do a certain thing on the grounds of technical ability. They talk as if rights stem more from what one can do than what one should do. Applying this way of thinking to human life, individuals have appropriated authority over life and death. Having become "like gods," they not only know the difference between good and evil—they claim the authority to define good and evil.

RESPONSE TO THE FALLACY:
Give the Author of life a chance and He'll tell you.

The nature of things

We have already discussed the meaning of nature and its inherent limits. The nature of nature, if you will, is to limit. But more than that, nature also orients. In other words, we are not at liberty to take the nature of things and arbitrarily alter it at our whim. The nature of things does not depend upon our desires or plans, but on reality—the way things are. To pretend things are any other way is not only to appropriate powers that do not belong to us, but even to create an unnatural world with all that this intrusion implies: frustration of natural ends, which ultimately means human frustration. (We're not just talking about biological nature, but about human nature and the natural ends of natural human acts.)

To know the nature of a faculty, one has to understand how it acts—and toward what end. The conjugal act has two natural ends: to bring about new life, and to augment and renew the union of love between the spouses.

Three's not a crowd, naturally

When the conjugal union is fertile, the consequence is more than just physical: a new human person appears on the scene. As we have previously seen, the human person is a composite of body and soul. The body is quite obviously the consequence of the physical union of the mother and father. But logic tells us that no effect can be greater than its cause; therefore, a spiritual reality cannot possibly be the effect of a physical cause. You don't get spiritual beings from physical action. In other words, human life is more than just the product of a man and a woman. It takes three to make a baby, and God is the one who supplies the soul.

God has entrusted to man's free collaboration elements of a plan that transcends man himself. Man takes the first initiative, willing the intimate union between spouses. This act, momentous in itself, is further elevated by the participation of God Himself in the moment of conception, when He creates the soul of the new human person. Taking into account that we are not God (and He is), it would seem logical, not to mention respectful, to allow Him to do what He wants, above all when dealing with such a weighty issue as human life. In a certain sense, we can say that the universe is altered with each new conception. God actively participates in the conjugal union and creates a new soul, someone who did not exist before, but, as we have seen, will exist forever. The conjugal act opens up an arena in which God might choose to act. God is free, but will respect our freedom even should we abuse it by unnaturally contracepting. Since it truly takes three to bring about human life, the contraceptive mentality slams the door in God's face and simply tells him, *You're not a part of this. You just watch.*

Woman: Is she who she is, or what she does?

If its disrespect toward God and His role in creation doesn't seem like enough to make contraception a bad idea, consider that it also furthers a destructive view of woman and human sexuality in general. The contraceptive mentality empties sex of significance: it's no longer receptive to new human life. Setting aside the physical dangers many contraceptives pose to the woman's body, consider the harm done to a woman's psychological well-being. Contraception leads women to believe that their fertility, no small aspect of their being, is an obstacle to their self-realization. Think about what a negative message men and women are getting. Both sexes come to see female fertility as an obstacle to what they want, so that womanhood itself is indirectly condemned.

A husband's total gift of himself and total acceptance of his wife with all that she is as a woman includes acceptance of her fertility. Through contraception, complementarity and interdependence of the sexes are done away with, and a substantial aspect of the woman is looked upon as an intrusive and unwanted.

One reason often given for use of contraception is to safeguard the woman's career. This choice subordinates openness to new life to material productivity. If woman's production is what is most esteemed, isn't it ironic that her most fruitful production is stifled and hidden as an embarrassing reminder of who she really is and what she is most uniquely capable of achieving? The woman's womb is by design a sanctuary that receives the smallest of seeds and gives back an everlasting human being with God's active collaboration.

Openness is not conditional

The spiritual element in man permits him to have dominion over himself and to give himself to another in love. This sincere gift of self, when it is reciprocated, can bring about a communion of two persons. This self-giving, when authentic, is reward enough for the lover; it reveals what it means "to lose oneself in order to find oneself." Total openness to one another means a total acceptance of the beloved in all that the beloved is and all that the unknown future holds for the two. Real openness of each spouse toward the other also ensures that one does not become a mere object of pleasure for the other. Both spouses find fulfillment in each other through this openness. Contraception interferes with this mutual openness. Thus artificial interventions that frustrate one of the natural ends of the conjugal act simultaneously frustrate the other end. Contraception prevents not just babies, but also bonding. Once deliberately robbed of its life-giving potential, the conjugal act ceases to be an act of love. To hold yourself back in the act of self-giving is not to give at all.

Nature as proper, not property

To claim openness to the spouse but not to the possibility of life is an oxymoron at best, a lie at worst. Contraception attempts to alter the meaning of human sexuality, and leaves both spouses short-changed. Since human nature is experienced as a condition and not as a free choice, man cannot claim the authority to rearrange it according to his own convenience. To destroy the original and ultimate meaning of human sexuality is to contradict human nature in man's most intimate human relationship. Just as your body does not belong to you, so too your nature is not counted amongst your belongings. And just as we experience limited authority over our bodies, so too do the limits of our nature extend to our souls, and to the marital relationship. It follows logically that man does not possess unlimited authority over his generative faculties.

Human sexuality is meant to serve the unitive aspect of marriage, and to this end it promotes the exclusivity and permanence of the marital union. But human love involves more than the unitive dimension. The unitive and procreative dimensions are coordinated. Both are integral to a harmonious concept of man. In other words, we cannot separate the sexual function from the person and treat it as something independent of the person. The human body is not merely an organ for sexual or other instinctual activities. It expresses the entire person. The human person, called to communion with another, experiences that communion most intensely when the two necessary elements of conjugal love—the unitive and the procreative—are present.

Openness to the possibility of life works as a reminder of how dependent upon exclusivity and permanence conjugal love and family life are. It is also a sign that the spouses are not merely interested in their own pleasure or satisfaction, but are genuinely committed to the good of the other in becoming one flesh, one heart, and one soul. Blocking the fertile dimension of the conjugal act strips the gift of self of its totality. The ethos of the conjugal act consists in authentically living all the dimensions of this gift according to the nature of the act, but—even more important—according to the nature of the human person who engages in it.

Back to radical individualism by way of matrimony? Thank you, no.

The true union between a man and a woman implies something more than openness to life. Life is nothing if there is not someone who lives. In other words, openness to life in the conjugal act is openness to this child who may be born of this particular union. Through marrying, a woman says, *You are uniquely valuable to me, and I want you to be the father of my children.* Contraceptive sex says, *I don't want you to be the father to my child. I don't want to be a mother. I don't want this child.* The truncated contraceptive union has only an immediate intention; it avoids a commitment to the long-term consequences of the natural marital union. Contraceptive sex, by the nature of its intention, could be shared with just about anyone. Such a mentality puts marriage and, therefore, happiness in jeopardy.

Ironically, contraceptive sex is practiced in the name of freedom and autonomy. But autonomy from the laws of the nature of things is not true freedom. It's chaos. Freedom cannot survive without truth, and love cannot survive without genuine freedom. Yet neither the laws of nature nor freedom itself is completely satisfactory to man. They are simply means, and means are not meant to satisfy but to help toward something greater. Through respect for nature's laws and living an authentic freedom founded upon truth, we achieve our ultimate goal: happiness.

Restless is our heart until it rests in Thee
Augustine Aurelius

Two loves built two cities: The earthly city by the love of self, even to contempt of God; The heavenly city by the love of God, even to contempt of self. The former glorifies in itself, the latter in the Lord.
Augustine Aurelius

I can't get no satisfaction.
Mr. Mick Jagger

FALLACY #25:

I can do whatever makes me happy!

Perhaps we never articulate it this way, but, in the end, all we really want is to be happy. This is normal. This is natural. But too often, in the name of personal happiness, we claim total autonomy and defend any and all behavior with *Just as long as it makes you happy . . .*

What's so fascinating about this theory (and practice) is that although we all share the same human nature we seem to be choosing radically different paths towards happiness.

Could we all be right?

RESPONSE TO THE FALACY:
Yes, but do you know what will make you truly happy?

Off kilter

I remember the summers of my youth when I was learning to play the Scottish Bagpipes. At the Highland Games I listened and watched the top pipers with awe: they played with such coolness and perfection and, at the end of the day, walked away with trophies, money, and my admiration. I can't deny having been somewhat envious. Then I discovered that with practice my fingers could do many of the intricate movements I had considered beyond me. I set goals for myself and strove to reach them. My piping improved. When a new tune caught my ear I couldn't think of anything else. My homework took a hike and even during class time I used to read the music as my head and heart wandered somewhere else. And each time I thought, *If I can just learn this tune with perfection, I will be content. I won't need any more. Once I learn this one, I've got it made.* But it was never that way. I always wanted another tune, a tougher one. The old tunes got older, and there seemed no end to my desire for more. The life lesson there for me was that there is no total satisfaction in this life. *I can't get no . . .*

Oh waiter, there seems to be a snail in my escargot

They say the best waiter is the one you don't notice or remember. I remember a waitress years ago who seemed to give our table preferential treatment. She not only wisely suggested that I order the house's own special version of "Campbell's Cream of Mushroom Soup"; she knowingly, even somewhat proudly, gave me a peek inside the chef's treasure trove of secrets: *Just add a smidgen more water than the label indicates.* Convinced that she had performed her duties as a waitress with unparalleled skill, and equally convinced that we would soon be on our way, since it was getting to be about closing time, our waitress surprised us by bringing us the check (tip included) and her life story (with many tips included). Not realizing how long this was going to take, I left my coat on. Dumb.

By the time we got to her early adolescence, I was getting a little hungry again.

It turned out that she had suffered a lot, fallen in with the wrong crowd in high school, began to take drugs, gotten pregnant, and considered suicide. Her father wanted her to abort the baby, but she said that her conscience wouldn't allow her. She recognized her many mistakes, but wasn't about to make that one. "It just wasn't right," she said. Her parents threw her out of the house shortly before the birth of their granddaughter; the mother-to-be had nowhere to go. She heard about a nun who helped girls in her situation and, feeling desperate, she humbled herself and asked for help. Thanks to the nun, her life changed radically. Not only was she able to save her unborn daughter; she was able to care for her without the worries involved in that life on the street. Throughout the process of purification she experienced, she began to know herself and accept her own worth, as well as all the accompanying responsibilities that human dignity demands. The experience of being on the receiving end of pure human love, perhaps for the first time, was exactly what she needed to "become more human," as she put it. But that wasn't all. She also realized that the love she was experiencing was only a weak reflection of God's infinite love which, in spite of its apparent hiddenness, had always been there for her, even when she couldn't spare Him a thought.

Then she began to pray.

Through prayer she allowed God access to her heart, and over time He went through a metamorphosis from being a pious legend in the back of her head to becoming the You of her life who gave her a reason to hope. Since the moment in which she made that act of courageous love toward her unborn child, her life has never been the same. She is now a good mother to her many children and strives to raise them to love God more than they love their very selves.

Nonetheless, she mentioned that, although she has a deep prayer life and has learned to be faithful to her conscience, she feels a longing for something more.

Naturally.

GOAL!

That is the universal experience. Everyone feels this longing for something more than the earthly experience of God, even the greatest of saints. Especially the greatest of saints experience the reality that this world is just not enough and the more we possess God in this life, the more we long to possess Him definitively and totally.

Think of the two examples we've just considered. A young man seeks happiness through something morally innocuous like the bagpipes and doesn't find it. A young girl seeks it through popularity, drugs, and promiscuity and doesn't find it. Where does one find it, anyway?

Consider the complexities of human history since the world began. History is multi-faceted, as is the life of an individual person. Yet one thing unites humanity, just as one thing unites the human person— our ultimate goal: happiness. We all seek whatever it is we seek because we want to be happy. Our hunger for happiness is what compels us to move toward that which we do not yet possess. All movement speaks of a good not yet attained, a striving for something, a yearning. Babies reach out for their mothers, children press their noses against candy store windows, men go to work each morning, old folks look for coins with metal detectors on California beaches. The baby wants more than milk, the child isn't ultimately satisfied with candy, man can't live on money alone, and retired people can dig as deep as they like in the sand, they won't find happiness there. It all comes down to achieving one's ultimate end. For human persons, happiness is the ultimate end of all human acts, the perfect good which alone satisfies human longing.

Happiness is about being good, not about being giddy

Happiness. It's the end for which we all we exist. But we don't all achieve it, and that's a shame. If Mick Jagger can't get no satisfaction it may be that he's looking in all the wrong places. The greatest human tragedy is the unhappiness resulting from an unfulfilled life. It's easy to *say* we're happy, but *are* we? We all seek happiness, complete happiness, but how many of us have truly found it?

If we believe ourselves to be totally happy, what is it that makes us so? Are the things that satisfy us things that are gong to continue into eternity along with our soul? If not, sooner or later we may join Mick in his sad refrain.

Does the one who dies with the most toys really win? What brings happiness and satisfaction? $$$$$$$$? Power? Health? Good looks? Good food and drink? Esteem?

You can claim that you find your satisfaction in food, or in sex, or in any other experience. But if that's the case, why does the longing for them always return after they have been had? None of those things can ever truly satisfy the needs of the human heart, because the human heart was made for much more. The human heart was made for even more than another human heart. Money, health, and looks are all goods of the body; but they all die with our bodies. And man is more than flesh and bone.

Man is made for more than earthly joys because man is greater than the earth. Man is spirit, and unless his spirit is satisfied, he will never find total peace and absolute happiness. But if man's soul means intellect and will, is happiness found in knowledge? Not necessarily. The particular goods of the soul, like knowledge or virtue, are a part of happiness, but not happiness itself. Even spiritual goods are concomitant goods; they merely accompany other necessary goods and are not sufficient to bring us complete happiness. We can only be satisfied with the best, with the greatest. Only God, the absolute good and ultimate end of man, can satisfy man's longing.

Those two faculties of the soul, the intellect and the will, are oriented toward truth and goodness, knowing and loving. As spiritual creatures, then, our fulfillment will only come through knowing and loving God. Of course we can't see Him as long as we are on Earth, but that's no excuse for not trying to get to know Him, trying to speak with Him, even loving Him. After all, human lovers who are separated from each other think about each other constantly and live faithful to each other in spite of physical distances. Their fidelity is part of their love for each other. We can do the same in our relationship with God. Although we can't see God with our physical eyes, we can know Him through prayer, we can love Him with all our heart, we can give ourselves to Him and allow Him to give Himself to us in an intimate act of love.

But why were we made in such a way that we can't see God while we remain on the earth? God is the absolute and ultimate end of all men. The minute we see Him, we experience total joy and neither need nor desire anything else. As they say, *To know Him is to love Him.* If we could see Him, we could never reject Him. (In case you were wondering, rejection of God is still called "sin.") But on this Earth we are given the opportunity to make a choice for God and, as long as we live, to choose Him by loving Him with all our heart, mind, and strength. Or we may freely choose not to love Him and, in doing so, reject Him. Since God is all good, He must also be all just. Therefore He respects our choice, with all of its consequences. If we choose Him, He's all ours and we're all His. If we do not choose Him . . . well, He respects that free decision, too. Is that unfair? Of course not. God respects our freedom, even when we abuse it. On the other hand, part of the thrill of loving God in the next life is finally seeing face to face the One we had chosen to love without ever having had a glimpse of Him on this Earth. Our free choice for God, lived out amidst many obstacles and often against the current of society, will not go unrequited.

In the last analysis, behind our choices for good or evil lies the eternal law in the mind of God that measures our choices. So it is quite logical that there be a direct relationship between our actions on this earth and our eternal reward. We all have the experience of blame and judgment: we call thieves and murderers bad and generous, responsible people good. We understand the justice of reward and punishment. To deny these facts is to imitate those mothers I run into after every summer camp who simply won't believe that their little angels could even have thought about misbehaving, much less acted badly. This refusal to face facts is based on self-deceiving sentimentalism, or simple dishonesty. God's judgments after our death are based not on some make-believe caricature, but on how we in fact did behave in this life. His judgment of us is as inescapable as reality itself; we cannot wish it away or send a memo stating that our lawyers will be in touch.

Morality impregnates every human act. And each human act speaks in varying degrees of gaining or losing temporal and eternal happiness. The life lived out to its fullest in the light of human reason (reflecting God's eternal law) opens itself to the possibility of achieving eternal happiness. Very different consequences can be expected from the life lived against the dictates of human reason and natural law.

We must be careful not to confuse our conscience and the inclinations of natural law with our whims and fancies. Following my conscience is not just about doing what I think is right, but about doing what truly is right—not about what I want, but what nature, allied with my reason, tells me I ought to do: in short, what God wants. To be faithful to one's conscience, one has to practice following it faithfully, as well informing it assiduously and correctly.

Inside us we find certain principles that are quite clear; there's no serious question about our behavior in some areas. But we also find other, fuzzier thoughts—and a myriad of voices besides that of our conscience: the voice of our society, the voices of our passions, the voices of fear and desire, and perhaps even Mom's voice still quite loud and clear within us. Amongst all of this interior traffic, how do we know what God wants us to do? An intelligent beginning would be to ask Him. That means becoming a prayerful person, in order to get to know God and, in knowing Him, find out what it is that pleases Him. Prayer is the moment in which we shut out all the other voices and speak with the One who loves us most and, perhaps more importantly, seek to hear His voice.

To live authentically, according to a conscience enlightened by the will of God, one has to have a lot of experience of asking questions about the moral rectitude of different acts. This means informing the conscience, forming it, and listening to it attentively. Immature persons often act without consulting the conscience, without asking, *Is this really a good thing to do?* Sometimes moral reflection goes no further than the promptings of social convention or the superficial reflexes of habit, regardless of their rationale. Only by listening to reason can we know what our duty really is. In the acceptance of the natural law as known through the reason, man finds himself equipped to begin the search for God's face. Reason is the faculty that, at our command, reaches out beyond the space-time limits of all creation toward the timeless and longed-for vision of God. If our quest is misguided and we never reach beyond ourselves or created goods, then we get what we asked for. The true good we experience in this life is an expansive, life-filling drive that readies our soul for the ultimate Good. Evil choices, on the other hand, ironically put constraints on man and truncate every aspect of his life, temporal and eternal.

We are recipients of a divine invitation to attach our smallness to God's greatness. And this is happiness. But the irony of it all is that we can't really understand this happiness, much less describe it, until we experience it.

Who says *you can't always get what you want*?

Normally, choosing eternal happiness is not something we improvise at the end of our lives. Love is not something we can conveniently switch on at our whim. In order to qualify as well-rooted love, our love for God requires a choice for our Beloved that has been renewed and ratified through sometimes-difficult-to-make individual choices over an extended period of time. Of course, one might have the chance to choose to love God in the last moment of one's life in order to possess Him in the next, but—apart from the risk that a deathbed repentance won't work out as planned—it is mercenary to give Him the crumbs of our last minutes, as a short-term investment in a sort of fire insurance policy.

To achieve this happiness one has to want it and to be willing to die for it. We would have no wheat if the grain of seed wheat had never fallen to the ground, been buried, and disappeared. Only if it dies does it bear fruit. So too with our earthly life. Death is the door to eternity, and we all have to pass through it. What awaits us depends in large part upon what we have done in this life, the choices we have made, where we have sought happiness, and how we have used our freedom.

If we keep things in their the proper order—freedom is a means best used in the light of truth, and happiness is our end—then we are on the right track. Man craves love more than power: Power is only an affirmation of who one is or believes oneself to be. Love, on the other hand, is something that we choose because of someone outside of ourselves; it makes us something more than we already are. And freedom is merely the condition for the choice. Love demands a gift of ourselves; freedom makes it possible. And the authentic recognition of truth makes freedom possible, because it is truth that differentiates between authentic goods and apparent goods, between what is sometimes mistakenly loved and what is truly lovely.

With disturbing and increasing frequency, I meet people who live in what is called *Bindungsangst*. This is a German word that, more or less, means fear of commitment. These people shun marriage vows, look with pity and incomprehension (and I suspect sometimes something of envy) upon priests and religious who have made vows and live up to them. They are incapable of understanding what patriotism means, they consider friendships as if they were business deals, and, in the event their intellect grants God existence, they only fear Him for what He may ask of them. The real irony of it all is that, in order to protect their precious freedom by never committing themselves to anything or anyone, they make themselves a walking prison and sentence themselves to a life-long term. They believe that, somehow, freedom to choose is a good best protected by not exercising it. If this view wins, love loses. But the person who truly loves, on the other hand, is not afraid of the consequences of a free choice for another person. More than anything else, he fears losing his beloved through a misuse of his own freedom—also known as infidelity. The one who is truly free is free to love, and to love without condition or limit. And unlimited, unconditioned love for God brings about unlimited, unconditional happiness.

The choice between the decision for love and true happiness, on the one hand, and, on the other, self-condemnation to the fear of love's consequences is the hinge upon which our happiness or unhappiness turns.

The waitress I introduced near the beginning of this chapter told us something before we parted that I will never forget. She ended her story by reminding us of who she had been and how low she had fallen, and that it was only through God's action in her life that she finally discovered her true identity as a child of God. She asked us to consider that every drug addict, prostitute, and poor soul that we see on the streets is an object of God's infinite love, who simply hasn't realized it yet.

For further information

God is our natural, ultimate end; and our moral life decides whether or not we will attain the vision and company of God for all eternity. But there's more to it than that. The possession of God implies a supernatural reality that goes beyond the scope of this book into the area of theology. This little book is concerned with what is accessible to human reason, which is a sufficient guide to man in the natural world of man, but falls short of divinely revealed truths. If man is to be led into the world of the supernatural, he must first be disposed to accept divine guidance. And that is the stuff of other books, written by greater men—such as Matthew, Mark, Luke, and John. If you are interested in what they have to say, read them. If you want to understand exactly what they say, pray along with them. And get in touch with the Catholic Church.

Epilogue

Although I have been able to address a small number of representative fallacies that are rampant in the First World (in which I include the U.S., Europe, and Canada), I'm convinced that the problem behind them all is not in the intellect, but rather in the heart. Therefore, any real fix for these fallacies is only cosmetic if it does not bring healing to the soul.

Once, when I was flying from Rome to New York, a cart-rolling stewardess interrupted a pleasant but unplanned nap to ask who had the Salisbury steak and who had the vegetarian plate. The 45-ish woman sitting next to me shrank back and looked somewhat disappointed at the question as she curtly let us all know that the "animal corpse" was not for her. I behaved myself and didn't pursue the discussion. During the course of the meal I had the feeling she was watching me from an interior distance, but I didn't make anything of it.

Then it happened.

I had just said a short prayer of thanksgiving after yet another Salisbury experience when she blurted out "I can't believe you!" I thought she was impressed with how fast I had integrated my lunch. I was wrong.

"Not only do you kill animals, you thank your god for it. How can you just pray in public like that and impose your worldview on people?"

"I thought I was imposing my worldview on the Salisbury steak," was my somewhat perplexed reply.

"I think your religion is a façade for intolerance and narrow-mindedness."

In an instant, I thought of all that might be behind her attitude: the almost hypnotic power of the mantra "tolerance," bad experiences she had perhaps unfortunately had with people acting in the name of religion, a conscience that had rejected God and was being pricked by an unexpected reminder of God's existence. I wasn't sure about the why's, but at 2:00 in the afternoon, I was more interested in a siesta than in investigating her ideology. I considered responding with a pastorally sensitive yawn and fading back into a nap. But I figured that such an answer doesn't really win people's hearts and minds.

The why's of her outburst kept nagging at me. Why is this thing called "tolerance" so intolerant? What makes people react to prayer and belief in God the way this woman did? I had the impression that she wouldn't be impressed with a yawn, no matter how sincere I made it. Yet, on the other hand, it was equally clear to me that an argument wasn't what she really needed, either.

Her reaction struck me as preprogrammed to the point of being automatic, machine-like. I had the impression that the only way an intelligent woman could embrace such knee-jerk attitudes was if they had been taught to her in a memorize-the-catechism fashion and assimilated through numerous repetitions. This plane trip certainly wasn't the first time I had experienced such a reaction to a manifestation of belief in God—or in any other absolute truth. The scientist I had the pleasure of meeting on my way to New York (you may remember him from the Introduction to this book), though more agreeable in his manner, held beliefs that necessarily lead to the very conclusions this angry woman was expressing.

So I asked her what was wrong. My query provoked a curt, "A lot." No doubt.

"Your intolerance of others and your church's oppression of women by making birth control *verboten*. How can you justify bringing a child into the world the way it is?"

Whether she knew it or not, I think there is a fundamental relationship between her targets of choice: tolerance and birth control.

"Tolerance" seems to have taken on a religious meaning. Whenever we hear the word, we intuit a liturgical rubric bidding, "All bow." Everyone is supposed to show respect for tolerance. And accusations of intolerance are supposed to be unanswerable. The beliefs of intolerant people are unworthy of expression. **Tolerance** has become so imposing a value that it appears incapable of allowing toleration for any person who would express (or "impose") any personal opinion not yet enjoying a stamp of approval from the cultural elite or Hollywood. This is how the woman on the plane took my saying a prayer before and after a meal.

Apparently it's a sin to express one's own personal belief even in silent prayer.

Why?

How can God offend someone who doesn't believe in Him—who thinks He doesn't even exist? You'd think prayer would seem merely futile, certainly not offensive, to a non-believer. Who's the chief offender here?

A prayer said in the inner sanctum of one's heart, accompanied only by some discreet external manifestation, offends because it reminds people of a reality that some consider offensive: the human person. The issue here is the human person himself. Only the offense some take at the human person can explain the relationship between unlimited tolerance and birth control. Nobody puts it exactly this way, but hatred of the human person is at the heart of what we might call the "tolerance-birth control mentality." The hatred that holds this world view together is not just a hatred of "those persons out there"; the hating person himself is not excluded from his own destructive passions. The human person, according to this view, uses up precious natural resources, puts animals in danger, kills and eats them, prays, passes on traditions, makes laws, punctures the ozone layer, gets in our way, makes demands upon us, and so forth. This human person, who is bad and certainly has no right to impose himself or his beliefs on us, is at his best when he simply, neutrally, undemandingly tolerates everything.

Why do intelligent Westerners despise Western culture and values? I have the impression that the reason is often a healthy sense of guilt for the objective personal sins of the individuals themselves, who—instead of changing their own ways—hope to find respite and reconciliation with themselves if they can just identify sinners even worse than they are. And then there's the fact that only the Catholic Church has consistently held up the fullest version of Western culture—and maintained the same moral teachings for the past 2,000 years. The Catholic Church stands as a beacon of light for all people, but not all desire to expose their actions to the light. People whose consciences cringe away from those moral teachings, but who nonetheless long for high ideals, accuse the light and reject the ideals, not willing to accept the obvious: the greater our own sins, the greater our need for such ideals.

We are proud creatures and find it difficult to forgive others, as well as ourselves. Either to ask forgiveness or accept it just seems to be too much for us. How could anyone deserve forgiveness? Who could earn it? Outside the context of forgiveness and redemption, there arises a natural psychological transference: instead of repenting our personal guilt, we blame everything on past or present totalitarians. And what makes the totalitarian, according to some, is intolerance.

Forgiveness and redemption cannot be earned or deserved. Nor can love. But regardless of merit, where there is love there is forgiveness, acceptance, and, quite obviously, babies. I guess we could say that Western culture dies if we are willing to abandon these three things: love, forgiveness, and babies—all of which really make sense only in the context of a personal relationship with God.

Much of modern thinking is staggering along a lonely road. It seems that we want to buy coexistence at the cost of the coexisting realities. The disappearance of the human subject follows from this radical concept of tolerance, which is not an affirmation of the human person, but rather the denial of his value, and even of his existence.

If tolerance means not recognizing objective values that were valid yesterday, are valid today, and always will be valid, then we must tolerate every dictator regardless of how intolerant he may be. Should we tolerate and acquiesce to a new Holocaust? Should we merely sit on our hands, being neither for nor against, content with the fact that we are not imposing our beliefs on anyone? What's the difference between tolerance . . . and cowardice?

We should not simply tolerate goodness—we should promote it. Nor should we tolerate evil. Silence gives consent. Adolf Hitler found too many tolerant people in his day, too many people who were not ready to take a decisive step to do good and oppose evil. Tolerance in this sense disarms good people before evildoers. Criminals are tolerated; the good, if merely tolerant, are neither really good (for the good choose the good, they do not just stand in front of it tolerating it) nor bad, just victims. And bland ones, at that.

A totalitarian is a totalitarian not because he does not tolerate, but because he does not respect the radical goodness of the human person. The so-called tolerant person collaborates with the totalitarian because he, likewise, refuses to accept the human person for what he is.

Our undervaluation of the human person produces a progressive darkening of man's capacity to discern the most fundamental of things: truth, goodness, beauty, love, forgiveness, and God. Man forgets who he is and why he was created and no longer sees himself as set apart from the rest of creation, but just as one more occupier of space on a planet filled with plants, water, and furniture. Life itself becomes merely an object over which we claim to have sovereignty—man takes it into his hands to control and manipulate. The eclipse of the sense of God has brought about this tragic vision of the human person, his dignity, and his life. The truth is that if we exclude God from the equation, we soon exclude ourselves.

Our hatred of ourselves explains why birth control is so rampant. We may claim noble reasons for contracepting, such as, "I couldn't justify bringing a child into the world the way it is"; but what we are actually saying is, "I wouldn't bring a child into the world the way I am." Our inability to affirm the radical goodness of the human person truncates love and twists it into a type of business deal, an exchange of goods and intentions sealed with a promise (sometimes) as a type of security. In contrast, the love that affirms the goodness of the person is an exchange not of properties but of persons. If I cannot affirm the goodness of the person (either the beloved or myself), I can never truly give myself in a definitive manner. If I can't affirm the goodness of any person, to whom would I want to give myself? And if I did find I loved somebody, why would I want to give myself to that person if I couldn't affirm my own goodness? True love not only makes this exchange of persons sealed with a vow possible, it also makes babies possible.

Not long ago, I had a conversation with several young couples. Trying to spare the wives from having to embarrass their husbands, I asked the men what had moved them to choose these women to be their wives, above the other 2.5 billion women of the world. One said he was captivated by her smile. Another said that the click came when he saw how she worked with children and concluded, *This woman would be a great mother to my children.* Still another said that he and his wife had a strong physical attraction that blossomed into a respect for each other's virtue and then became true friendship.

All of the reasons were sincere, valid, and beautiful. And the couples are happily married amidst the normal difficulties every couple must undergo. Yet how often do we reduce love to *What's in it for me?* We may not articulate it that way, but our love is almost always tainted with at least a shadow of self-seeking. There usually is something in it for me. After all, I decide if I like her smile, her brains, her ability to raise children, then I'm choosing what I think would be good for me.

So the question remains: Is a totally selfless love possible? Yes, and your existence is proof of it.

God created you out of nothing. Why? Now there's a question . . . Because of your good looks? Because you've got a great personality? But who gave you your looks and your personality—and everything else that makes you lovable? If we think we're deserving of God's love, then we haven't understood His creation, or Him, at all.

When a young man falls in love with a girl, he discovers something good in her, something beautiful in her that moves him to love that goodness and beauty. That is human love, and it is wonderful. But when God considered you for the first time, you did not even exist except as a possibility. There was absolutely nothing there that could have made Him fall in love with you.

Can you fall in love with one of your own imaginings? Why did God create you? All you have and all you are are His gifts; He had absolutely nothing to gain in creating you. In fact, He had plenty to lose. There, written between the lines, is our answer: God created you for no reason at all. His creating act was motivated by no reason. Now, an act so performed is perfectly disinterested. He created you, nonetheless, with the desire that you be the recipient of His love and that you respond to it freely. He contemplated you from eternity, fell in love with this image of you, and decided to make you a reality. The being that you call "Me" was not created because you did something to deserve it. Your very personhood is a pure gift—and proof of God's love for you. Your existence is the argument for your radical goodness. He created you simply because He loved you and thought it would be wonderful to be loved by you. No other reason could constrain God to create you.

While the answers to our culture's difficulties often seem complex, the truth is not complex. We are. To be able to formulate the correct answers is a good thing. And to live according to the truth is better. But knowing and loving God is truly living.

Glossary

ABSTRACT IDEAS: See **ABSTRACTION**. See also **UNIVERSAL IDEAS**.

ABSTRACTION: From the Latin word *abs-trahere*, which means to separate. Abstraction is the operation or set of operations with which the intellect forms a universal concept. It is the process by which one passes from a concrete sensible thing to an intelligible abstract thing (a concept). I see a dog, and from this experience of a particular thing I form the concept of "dog" in order to better recognize other dogs in the future. Abstraction interiorizes things in the form of concepts. Certainly the intellect forms concepts starting from material reality. Still, the concept, thanks to its universality, does not remain bound and dependent on matter: it begins from matter, but it transcends matter and the sensible world. The intellect depends extrinsically on sensibility, but not intrinsically. I know this doesn't seem to affect your life at all and doesn't seem the least bit important. But it is. Trust me.

ACT: That which changes something else and brings it to perfection.

ADJUNCT WILL: When the intellect recognizes the veracity or the goodness of something and the will consequently acts, we call this an adjunct will. In the case of God's adjunct will, we recognize that

His intellect and His will are only analogically distinct from each other. Nonetheless, He can know beings as possible beings without bringing them into existence. But when He knows a possible being and His will decides to bring it into existence, we say His will is adjunct.

AGNOSTICISM: An unliveable theory that asserts that man cannot rationally assent to God's existence or non-existence. At the end of the day, we all live either as if God exists or as if He doesn't.

ANNIHILATION: This is the opposite of creation. The Latin word *nihil* means "nothing," so annihilation means reducing something to non-being. Since only God can create the human spirit, only God can annihilate it. Some people believe that the human soul no longer exists after death. This belief contradicts logic: only material things can wear out or get rusty; spiritual realities cannot suffer material damage. If only God can create a soul, then it seems logical that only God can destroy one. On the other hand, the destruction of a soul would be a contradiction of the divine will that created the soul, and this contradiction would be an imperfection in God, and a divine imperfection would put God out of a job.

ANTHROPOLOGY: See **PHILOSOPHY OF MAN**.

APPETITE: Appetite comes from the Latin, *appetere*, meaning *petere ad*, or directing oneself toward something else. A tendency is more than an inclination; it suggests an activity that has an end. The tendency or appetite can arise immediately from the nature of a being, without any type of previous knowledge: this kind of tendency we call "non-psychic." But if a tendency arises through an "elicit" act of sensitive (or intellective) knowledge, then we have a sensitive (or intellective) tendency.

ATHEISM: A choice freely made against belief in God. Often this choice is made to assert a sort of lonely dignity for man, which, it is claimed, would not exist if God did.

BEING: That which gives existence to all that is. If something exists, it is because it has being. So we can say that being is the highest of all perfections, limited only by the particular nature of the thing in existence that enjoys being. Being is what all existing things have in common.

BELIEF: A choice to accept the validity of a claim—usually made more on the weight of the source than on the content of the claim. Faith-choices of this kind are made all day, every day, by everybody, on many different levels of human experience. To get on an airplane is to make an act of faith on a natural level. The faith is more in the people entrusted with the care and flight of the airplane than in the airplane itself. The act of getting on the plane says, *I trust these people know what they are doing; they certainly know more than I do. I choose to take this flight.* The choice to believe is also made on more existential levels, such as in the area of morals and on the supernatural level of religion.

CAUSALITY: When causality is efficient, it is relational, in that one being, the cause, acts upon another being, the effect, to bring about some change. Some people deny causality, all people live by it. See also **PRINCIPLE OF CAUSALITY**.

CAUSE: That which by its action produces something else which, inasmuch as it is produced, is an effect.

CERTAINTY: Wimps fear it. Certainty means commitment because it means a recognized truth, and a recognized truth constrains us to live in accordance with it. We often hear people say they can't be certain about some moral question; they feel that their doubt liberates them from the consequences of the truth. Not so, not so.

We affirm all sorts of things with certainty: it's cold out, that is a car, and so forth. We affirm those things without the least fear of being contradicted because they are capable of being known. And so too are those inconvenient moral truths we'd rather not recognize.

COMMON NONSENSE: Fad-like ideological theories which claim victims by inducing people to jettison logic, truth, and other superfluous intellectual baggage.

COMMON SENSE: The common root of all the senses; their convergence into a common deposit and stockpile of learned experience and simple logic. Often the least common of all the senses.

COMPLEMENTARITY: A healthy recognition of the true diversity between men and women, which respectfully allows them to fulfill themselves through their natural and diverse tasks as husband and wife, father and mother. Complementarity in no way suggests a diversity of value in the man and woman or in their tasks, but a relationship in which each is a completion and counterpart for each other.

CONCEPT: An abstract expression of the nature of something. Once you know what a tree is, through your experience of a tree or many trees, you are now qualified to come up with the concept of "tree" in your mind. The tree in your backyard can become overgrown, grow diseased, or be chopped down, but the concept of tree stays the same forever. The concept is interior; it is manifested externally by means of the word. Oral or written words capture concepts and make them communicable to others. Concepts are our friends.

CONSCIENCE: A practical judgment of human reason concerning the moral goodness or evil of an action. This is an act of the intellect in collaboration with the will. The conscience does not close man in on himself, but opens him to the voice of God. Here is the entire mystery as well as the dignity of the moral conscience: it is the sacred place where God speaks to man.

CONSCIOUSNESS: From Latin, *cum-scire*, concomitant knowledge. Consciousness is reflexive: Man not only thinks, but he knows he thinks. He is able to enter into himself and think of his own thinking. In other words, I perceive myself, my thought as an act, and the contents of my thought; and I think about them. It sounds more complicated than it is, but we do it all the time. In reflexive consciousness, the attention is placed first on the subject, without distinguishing itself from the object. In the animal, consciousness is rapport with the world, but not rapport with oneself. Man's knowledge is a rapport with the thinker himself.

CONTINGENT BEINGS: Beings dependent upon a cause for their own existence. See also **EFFECT**.

CREATION OF THE SOUL: God directly and immediately creates the soul of each man. The principle of causality tells us that we cannot achieve a greater effect from a lesser cause. Applying this principle to the human person, we find that the biological conjugal act is insufficient to bring about the creation of a spiritual reality. You can't give what you don't got. Nor can the soul proceed from any pre-existing spiritual substance; spiritual substances are simple and cannot change from one into another. So it follows that the soul of each man must have been created from nothing. And since creation is an effect and there are no effects without causes, the soul must be a direct creation of God.

CULPABLE IGNORANCE: See **IGNORANCE**.

DIVERSITY: The fact of differences amongst different people. Diversity is merely a fact and not necessarily a value or virtue. Marriage requires diversity of sexes for the fruitfulness and authentic union of the spouses, which are the two ends of marriage.

EFFECT: See the definition for **CAUSE** but read it backwards. Thank you.

EMOTION: See **SENTIMENT**.

EMPIRICISM: A dogma of scientific faith. Empiricists claim that experience is the only source for human knowledge and the only criterion for the truth of the judgments of the intellect, which are valid only if they can be scientifically proven. See also MATERIALISM.

EQUAL: See **EQUALITY**.

EQUALITY: Similarity or sameness. On the human level, all men are equal in that they share human nature and therefore have the same worth.

EQUAL HUMAN DIGNITY: If all men are the same in the order of worth, they are not necessarily so according to the other orders. Not everybody deserves the same treatment: society should treat criminals differently from innocent people; parents may have to spend more money on sick children than on their other healthy ones. To uphold justice, society should recognize legitimate differences.

ESSENCE: See NATURE.

ETHICS: The science that guides our judgment concerning the morality of human acts.

EVERLASTING LIFE: This is the experience of purely spiritual beings presently, and of human souls after human death. Time has a beginning and an end, and God has no beginning and no end. But created spiritual beings experience a beginning, though no temporal end. All human souls, upon death, go into everlasting life to receive rewards or punishments for their actions on earth.

EVIL: A lack of something appropriate; the opposite of good; the ontological equivalent of non-being. Evil does not exist of itself, but only in concrete substances, without which it would not be thinkable. Evil does not exist, but there exist privations in subjects. For example, there is no falsehood, just false statements, no ugliness itself but, yes, ugly things. Paradoxically, evil is related to good and cannot be comprehended without reference to good. On a moral level evil is called "sin."

EXCLUSIVITY: The act of self-giving in marriage, to be authentic, must be a total gift of self. The nature of marital love requires that it never be shared it with any partner outside of the marriage covenant. Total self-giving means a decision for the beloved, which is necessarily an exclusive commitment.

EXISTENTIAL: Having to do with the primary act of existing. Sound philosophers correctly maintain that existentialism means the relation of the act of existing to the nature of the existent being, by whom freedom is obtained through wise use of the intellect. Bad philosophers hold that the primary act of existing destroys nature and intelligibility. Shame on them . . . at their age.

EXTERIOR SENSES: Sight, hearing, smell, taste, and touch: our means of obtaining authentic knowledge of material realities. They are called exterior senses because they operate in our sensory nerves, rather than in our minds. See also **INTERIOR SENSES**.

EXTRINSIC: Not intrinsic. Therefore, not a fundamental characteristic of any subject.

EXTRINSICALLY: See **EXTRINSIC**.

FAMILY: Man is a social being as well as a product of the most intimate and primordial society: the family. This conjugal union is established through the consent of a man and a woman. Their union is ordered to their own good as well as the good of the children who will come about as a result of their intimate union. Thus the man and woman are responsible for the needs of their children, and of each other. The institution of marriage is prior to any state, government, or judicial body; such bodies have no authority to alter the identity or definition of the natural human family.

FREEDOM: See **FREE WILL.**

FREE WILL or **LIBERTY OF CHOICE:** These are some often misunderstood and even abused terms. Free acts are obviously dependent on man's ability to act freely to choose one thing over another, or to simply opt not to act at all. The will plays a key role in the free human act, in that the will decides how and whether or not to act. The intellect, on the other hand, plays a different role: it considers the options, and having considered them, hands the decision over to the will, which acts. Each act is not only a choice, but also an act of self-definition for the acting person. Freedom of choice allows the human person to realize himself. But to accept the fact of self-definition and self-realization through free acts is to accept a moral norm for action. We all recognize the difference between good and bad. These terms make sense only if in fact men can act freely, and in turn do things that are objectively good or bad. A state prison speaks of human worth and dignity because punishment for crime respects the human person's freedom to choose whether to be good or bad—even to define himself as criminal. If a man commits a crime, he abuses his freedom and acts in a way that's beneath his dignity. Society respects the natural law and recognizes that, although a criminal is called to realize himself through free acts, he has chosen freely to act in an evil way and has lost something of his dignity. Justice speaks of freedom, and freedom speaks of good and evil.

GOOD: That which is fulfilling, and therefore desirable. There are both sensible and intelligible goods. Sensible goods appeal to physical and emotional desires, while intelligible goods help man become what he should be.

GOODNESS: See **GOOD**.

HABIT: From the Latin *habere,* to have, to possess, and, perhaps more directly, from *habitus,* an acquired tendency. A faculty is what permits us to act at all; a habit is what allows us to act more efficiently and with more ease in a determined way. Habits, depending upon their direction, can be good or evil. A habit is the product of free choices that define the human person. A habit may be lost through the practice of a contrary habit.

HAPPINESS: This is the end of all human activity, what every human being longs for. Happiness is the end result of human fulfillment. Since human happiness is found in the fulfillment of the person, it is clear that there must be a direct relationship between human happiness and human goodness. The good things that fulfill the human person are actually aspects of the person, as opposed to realities apart from the person. Things we own can help us to a certain type of practical fulfilment, but our ultimate happiness is not dependent upon our possessions. We experience happiness on many different levels of human existence. But it is the attainment of higher goods that makes the enjoyment of subordinate goods either possible and meaningful—or else needless. Happiness is the legitimate end of all aspects of the person. Both goods of the body and goods of the soul contribute to human happiness. Since the soul will last longer than the body, the most important goods are those that ensure the eternal happiness of the soul. Enjoying God's presence in eternity is the ultimate happiness, since it is the complete fulfillment of man's intellect and will.

HEDONISM: A distorted view of man that confuses human fulfillment with the experience of pleasure and the absence of pain.

HUMAN ACTS: These are acts that arise from free will. Man is not simply the cause of them, but is the *free* cause of them, in that they require consciousness and liberty of action. The flow of blood through the veins, unconscious blinks, and even those acts committed under psychological pressure of some sort are not truly human acts. Human acts require the collaboration of the intellect and the will, and have three parts: deliberation, judgment (or counsel), and choice. The intellect is the protagonist of the first two, and the will takes over in the third.

HUMAN DEATH: One day the funeral is going to be for you. There is a unity of body and soul which form the human person, but with the divorce of body and soul, the soul goes into everlasting life and the body remains on earth a short while until it is no more. The body is not a human person anymore, and neither is the soul. It is not correct to say that only the body dies: the man dies, even though the soul perdures forever.

HUMAN KNOWLEDGE: Human knowledge can be synthesized in one word: *thought.* Man thinks. This is a process in three acts: conceptualization, judgment, and reason. Man, beginning from the data of the external senses, forms concepts.

1. **Conceptualization**: I glance out my window and see a dog. With wonder and awe, I utter, "Dog." First step.
2. **Judgment**: I put that concept "dog" together with another concept. "That dog is eating something." Second step.
3. **Reason:** I bring several judgments together to come to a reasoned conclusion. "That dog eats, I eat, and therefore I eat that dog." The results of this process are not guaranteed, but the process itself is what interests us here.

This mental process is proper to man, and no animal is capable of it. These three acts suppose that man has the capacity of abstraction that is proper and specific to the human intellect. By the way, if you're a little down because your pets don't go to Heaven, just think, for an act of disobedience your dog could have spent an eternity in Hound Hell or several thousand years chasing his tail in Puppy Purgatory. So it's not so bad after all.

HUMAN NATURE: The human body carries its own interior vitality within itself: namely, the soul. The human body is "human" inasmuch as it is interiorly animated by the soul. That's why we call dead bodies corpses and not persons. Human bodyliness presents us with the body and the spirit together in an indissoluble unity: the man. Bodyliness is the specific mode of existence of the human spirit: the body reveals the man, expresses the person. Certainly, man is a person thanks to the spirit, because the person is essentially spiritual: only he who is gifted with a spirit (with an intellectual nature) is a person. But man is not a pure spirit, nor pure matter, but rather an enfleshed spirit. Naturally.

HUMAN PERSON: From the Latin *personare*, which means "to make resound on all sides." Man is a corporeal and spiritual being. As corporeal, man is a material individual. As spiritual, man has a rational nature endowed with a free will. His rationality gives man openness to being, for rationality is the root from which liberty, vocation, and love come—all of which are manifested in human acts. As a spiritual being worthy of freedom, each man is allowed to determine his own fate.

HUMAN SEXUALITY: Sexuality is not confined to generative acts, or a single function. Sexuality is something that is expressed throughout one's life, in almost every human act. Although there is only one human nature, it has two expressions: male and female. The sexuality of a person defines that person's behavior and psychology. So a man is different from a woman not only physically, but also psychologically. A woman is a woman on every plane of her existence. The differences between the sexes mean complementarity more than conflict or incompatibility. In its fullest expression—in the complementarity of the sexes and the mutual help they give one another—sexuality brings about new life and increased love between a man and a woman, thus ensuring the continuation of the species as well as the fulfillment of both spouses. The meaning of human sexuality is found in the intersubjective and interpersonal encounter between human beings of opposite sexes. The intersubjectivity between a man and a woman becomes total in an act of total self-giving, which requires a certain context of permanence, stability, and exclusivity. In human sexuality one is dealing not only with a function but with the whole human being; not only with a particular activity but with the realization of man as man. Therefore human sexuality cannot be localized or limited to genitality; it is a global dimension of the person, a dimension that is psychic as well as physical. Sexuality embraces the whole person.

IGNORANCE—INVINCIBLE, VINCIBLE, WILLED, CULPABLE, and **INCULPABLE**: All of these are problems of the conscience that differ in their moral consequences. An invincibly ignorant conscience is a conscience that, ignorant for some innocent reason, approves an objectively evil act. Invincible ignorance can be corrected through better information and formation of the conscience. The vincibly ignorant conscience is one in which the person takes no trouble to find out what is good or bad before acting. This is a moral problem. The culpably ignorant conscience is the worst of the three, in that the person acts knowing full well that what he is doing is wrong.

IMMORTALITY: Simply immunity from corruption. We can call those personal and conscious beings that exist outside of the limits of space and time immortal. We can apply this attribute to God's nature since He cannot not exist. But we can also apply it to the human soul, which is by nature not dependent upon the body for its acts and attributes and life.

INCULPABLE IGNORANCE: See **IGNORANCE.**

INDIVIDUAL: Any substance which of itself forms an integral whole.

INDIVIDUALISM: Man is social by nature. He is attracted to human company. Because the human person has a soul, he is open to others and for others. This openness is part of the very structure of human nature. This openness to other intelligent beings makes man a relational being able to come into contact with others and have an intersubjective rapport with them. Individualism contradicts this quality in man. Certainly, man determines his own identity through his choices, but individualism stresses this truth in an exaggerated way and sacrifices intersubjectiviy for the interests of the individual. We experience intersubjectivity in four forms: love, justice, conflict, and indifference.

INSTINCT: From the Latin *instinguere,* to push, to instigate. An innate, specific tendency that does not require the intellect or the will, but pushes the individual to perform a given activity. Instincts are inherent tendencies that arise naturally and spontaneously from the nature of a being. Human beings and animals have instincts.

INTELLECT: See **MIND.**

INTERIOR SENSES: Those senses confined to the interior of the human person, such as the imagination and the memory.

INTERSUBJECTIVITY: See **INDIVIDUALISM.**

INTRINSIC: Fundamentally characteristic of any subject.

INTRINSICALLY: See **INTRINSIC.**

INVINCIBLE IGNORANCE: See **IGNORANCE.**

JUSTICE: A principle that respects the truth of who man is, and in doing so, demands rights as a consequence. Justice stems from man's social nature and governs his interactions, obliging him to give others their due and ensuring that he receives his due. If we consider that justice concerns giving each his due and also consider the varied relations men have with one another, then the different facets of justice become clear. Toward his Creator man owes a justice called religion. Toward his parents, man owes the justice of piety (filial respect). Toward his superiors, in the name of justice, man owes obedience. And toward every sort of benefactor, man owes gratitude.

KNOWLEDGE: See **HUMAN KNOWLEDGE.**

LOGICAL TRUTH: See **TRUTH.**

LOVE: A tendency to a known good (for one cannot love what one does not know). There is no love without an object to be loved. Love tends toward union with the beloved. It is a union in which the lover is transformed by and in a certain way even converted into the beloved. Insofar as it transforms the lover into the beloved, love makes lovers interpenetrate one another, so that nothing that belongs to the beloved remains foreign to the lover. Experience teaches us that man cannot realize himself fully except in gift and communion with another. Love is the act that realizes the person in the most complete way. One might claim to love something that is objectively evil, but this love is simply an appreciation of a distorted good. Love of an authentic good makes man good, elevates him, and leads him to self-perfection. Love of merely apparent but false good degrades man and brings about an interior disintegration in man that sometimes has exterior effects. Thus love is the basis of moral action. It is love, in the ultimate analysis, that determines the quality of an action and of the person who performs it. The fulfillment that comes about as a result of love is true human freedom. If we do not love authentically, we cannot be authentically free.

MANIFESTATION OF TRUTH: See **TRUTH.**

MARRIAGE: As a fundamental aspect of the natural law, we can claim that marriage is not the work of man, but transcends him. Through marriage a man and a woman establish a covenant of love with each other in which they commit themselves to live together in fidelity—which means stability, permanence, exclusivity—for their own good and the good of their children.

MATERIALISM: The belief that everything can be reduced to matter and physical—even chemical—phenomena. The materialist understanding of man consists in the denial of the spirit and transcendence, and is based on the conviction that matter is the matrix of all reality. According to the materialist, man may be the most elevated expression of evolving matter, but although he manifests a level of existence that is profoundly different from that of the animals, he is comprehensible and reducible to material categories alone; psychic phenomena are nothing but the most elevated state of evolving matter. Isn't that refreshing? See also **EMPIRICISM.**

MATERIALISTS: See **MATERIALISM.**

MIND: The act of thinking is proof of the existence of the human soul. Obviously you can't give what you don't got. Likewise, you can't paint a picture without paint. (How's that for profound philosophy? But if that's not enough, read on.) The human soul has several faculties. We discover the soul first through its acts: primarily, through thought. The intellect in act is not totally dependent upon matter. Our concepts are not material, but spiritual. In order to produce spiritual concepts, the being that produces them must be spiritual in itself. If the mind were confined to the world of matter, it would only be able to know according to matter. But it isn't, so it doesn't. We are capable of knowing things apart from matter—justice, freedom, love, and so forth. We should be careful not to think the intellect is restricted to the brain in the same way as smelling is confined to the nose: we may have smelly feet, or even smelly noses, but we will never have smelling feet. The brain, like the nose, is material, but the intellect is not restricted to the brain because something material cannot possibly produce something spiritual. The cause of all intellective knowledge is the intellect, while the brain is merely the condition for our knowledge. An important condition, but just a condition, nonetheless.

MOE, LARRY & CURLY: In various philosophical systems we find references to the transcendentals: truth, unity, and goodness, all of which exist in each individual thing that exists, not as distinct parts of the being, but as distinct approaches to it. The three myth-like figures Moe, Larry & Curly embody the transcendentals on the level of human experience.

MORAL EVIL: Sin. Yes, sin. This is a bad choice made contrary to a moral norm. Evil cannot be understood outside of the concept of good, of which evil is a privation. And moral evil is a privation of virtue in a human person. Through moral evil the human person becomes something less and loses his dignity, though not his worth.

MORAL JUDGMENT: A judgment about the objective morality of a human act in a concrete situation. Moral judgments involve the consideration of all the conditions that affect the morality of an act: the nature of the act itself, the purpose of the acting person, and its circumstances, including ignorance, fear, concupiscence, violence, habit, temperament, and nervous mental disorders.

MORALS: Human conduct in light of ethics. One may have pristine ethics, but bad morals.

MORAL VALUE: Not a product of the individual conscience but a standard for the conscience's judgement of the goodness or badness of an action. There is a subjective element of the conscience in that the human person recognizes the judgments of the conscience as his own. But the conscience judges by a standard outside of itself, which is objective. This standard is moral value.

NATURAL APPETITES: Surprisingly, those appetites corresponding to our nature. Amongst them we number the inclinations to nourishment, sleep, procreation, and so forth.

NATURAL LAW: This is the law that is written on each man's heart and that shows him the way to follow so as to practice the good and attain his end. By the light of reason man knows what he must do as well as what he must avoid. It is an immutable law, permanent throughout history, subsisting under the flux of ideas, customs, and technological progress.

NATURAL RIGHT: Natural rights have to do with others' responsibilities toward an individual because of his nature. All have a right to what is most basic to their nature: life, nourishment, education, safety, and so forth.

NATURE: Nature means what something is. A chair is not a mongoose by nature, but a chair. The nature of a thing defines how it acts. You will find it more comfortable to sit on a chair than on a mongoose. Our recognition of the nature of a thing determines what we do with it, how it should be treated, and so forth. To deny nature, although it may be in vogue, is wishful thinking. We couldn't survive without natural distinctions such as the difference between water and poison, between a pincushion and a grizzly bear. Nature is the same thing as essence, but the word "nature" highlights the dynamic principle that moves the being to a certain type of action or use. See also **HUMAN NATURE.**

NECESSARY: That which must be so—for example, a first mover or first cause.

OBJECT: A Latin word *obiectum*, which means to be in front of. Subject and object appear opposed to each other with something intermediate between them, which is the psychic act by which the subject knows the object, and by which the object is mentally presented to the subject.

ONTOLOGICAL: Comes from the Greek *ons, ontos*, which means being and is synonymous with the word "entity."

ONTOLOGICAL TRUTH: See **TRUTH.**

PARTICULAR: One individual existing thing—Mr. Sniggles, my next door neighbor, for example—as opposed to a universal concept— humanity, for instance. The particular participates in the universal concept. Human nature exists in all human beings, but of itself humanity does not exist. Mr. Sniggles does exist and so he is a particular. And a very nice particular at that.

PASSION: A particularly strong tendency in a determined direction. Passions get stronger with their exercise (or lack of control). Depending upon their object, they can be good or evil.

PERCEPTION: The knowing process that presents objects sensibly to us in a complete and unitary form. Perception is a set of capacities and acts by which we not only apprehend sensible objects, but we apprehend them in an ordered, configured, and structured whole. When you glance up in the sky and see an airplane, you take in the whole image of the plane as it is through perception.

PERFECTION: The total lack of lack. Something is perfect when it possesses all that it needs to complete its nature.

PERMANANCE: The act of self-giving in marriage, in order to be authentic, must be a total gift of self. The nature of human love as total gift of self precludes attempts to rupture this covenant. Marriage means more than a contract between two people; it is a covenant that transcends each one of them, and even both of them together. The element of stability is inherent in marriage, given all that the commitment to the spouse implies: accepting the beloved with everything that makes up that individual's life and person, with each spouse sharing the other's destiny.

PERSONAL IMMORTALITY: The human soul is immortal. Because the human soul was directly created by God and because it is evident that man can have a rapport with his creator that other creatures cannot, we can reasonably conclude that God wills man's existence in order to have a rapport with him. Otherwise, we never would have been given the ability to do so. God created the human person in order to have a loving relationship with Him, which requires immortality. God could not will a man into existence as a means since love excludes using the beloved as a means, so man must be an end in himself. To will someone into existence in order to love him and to be loved by him implies the will that the beloved always exist. God does not offer his love on a time-share basis. Love means *I want you as a part of my life.* God's life is eternal, so His love and our response to it go far beyond limits of time and space.

PHILOSOPHY: A word that comes from two Greek words that together mean "love of wisdom." Aristotle raised this term to a verb and pointed out that "to say that one cannot philosophize, is to philosophize." In other words, *If you think you can't think . . . what's your problem?*

PHILOSOPHY OF MAN: The philosophical discipline that considers the entire man and investigates the existence and the nature of the first principles of his being and his acting by means of critical reflection on man's acts. You can call this "anthropology" to impress your neighbors.

PHYSICAL EVIL: Pain or any other privation experienced because of a lack of something that should be there.

POLYANDRY: The unnatural society of one wife with more than one husband. Which one's Dad?

POLYGAMY: The unnatural society of one man with more than one wife. Usually polygamy refers to a plurality of coincidental wives but, given the permanent nature of marriage, it can also mean having successive wives.

POSITIVE LAW: Those laws made by man, unlike the law written upon the heart of man by God. Nonetheless, positive law should uphold the higher natural law and ratify it. If a positive law contradicts the natural or revealed law, no man must comply with it. To allow positive law to defy or ignore the natural law is to allow human lawmakers to re-define man.

POSSIBLE BEING: A possible being is something that could exist, but doesn't yet, and may never exist. Its very existence does not present any logical contradictions. Flies exist, so do accordions. Perhaps it's not unthinkable to come up with a flying accordion. But you couldn't come up with a fly that is an accordion. That would be impossible.

POTENCY: The principle of change in a being. Potency is ordered towards actualization.

PRACTICAL: Usually refers to a type of intellect that has to do with concrete knowledge: how much sand to mix with the water and cement, for example. Ethics is the most practical of all studies.

PRINCIPLE OF CAUSALITY: If we find the reason for something's existence in itself, then it is self-causing. But we know that there are things whose existence is dependent upon something or someone else. There are things that could exist, yet do not. Whatever brings something else into existence is called its cause. The cause of anything is found outside of that thing. So all beings that have come into existence require an exterior cause for their very existence. All that exists has a sufficient reason for its being. To get to this principle, we first of all make the inescapable assumption that reality is knowable. (To deny this is intellectual suicide.) And if things are knowable, then there must be a reason for them. Further, this reason must also be knowable. Since all reality is made up of that which does or can exist, then there must be a reason for everything that does or can exist. See also CAUSALITY and CAUSE.

PRINCIPLE OF IDENTITY (AND **PRINCIPLE OF NON-CONTRA-DICTION**): *Roses are red, violets are blue, I'm schizophrenic and so am I.* You are you. That is the principle of identity. If you have difficulties with that, you need more help than this book can give. Since you are you, you are not your dad—or anyone or anything else that isn't you. That's the principle of non-contradiction. What is cannot not be at the same time.

PRINCIPLE OF NON-CONTRADICTION. See **PRINCIPLE OF IDENTITY**.

PURE ACT: The perfection in unchangeability. This is a total lack of potentiality that does not admit any limitations and of itself is unlimited self-realization.

RATIONALISM: The belief that only those ideas that can be grasped by the human intellect are worthy of being called true.

REAL BEING: A real being is something that exists. See also **POSSIBLE BEING**.

REASON: A concept is an immaterial existent, an idea free from space-time limitations: the idea of "man," for example, or of "mortality." A judgment is the joining of two concepts to come up with a true statement: "Man is mortal." Reason takes several judgments and links them together through logic to come to a rational conclusion: "You are a man. All men are mortal. Therefore, you're mortal."

RELATIVISM: The doctrine that it is always and absolutely true that there is never any absolute truth. All knowledge and truth are dependent upon time and place, individual and experience. Harrumph.

REVEALED LAW: Those laws made known to man by God's divine intervention.

RIGHT: Rights do not exist except in relation to duties, which are the social aspects of one's legal and moral responsibilities. A right is an attribute of a person or group that corresponds to a responsibility that someone else has toward that individual or group. Rights affirm the dignity of man as an end in himself. And that, by the way, explains why animals can never have rights—since they are means. Since each man is an end in himself, and yet there are as many ends in themselves as there are men on the earth, we need positive law that regulates the activities of men and the use of things in common. Different states in life amongst men bring with them different rights and responsibilities.

SENTIMENT: A sentiment is a purely subjective aspect of psychic life that consists in the pleasant or unpleasant impression that the psychic life produces in the subject through impressions or images, whether of thoughts or of real objects. An emotion is an intense sentiment that brings about physical changes: an increase in the heart rate, tears, laughter, and so forth.

SIMPLE: See **SIMPLICITY**.

SIMPLICITY: Rather than a defect, simplicity implies unity, integrity and perfection. Simplicity, as opposed to complexity, means not being a made up of composite parts, or not requiring externals for one's perfection. Pure spirits are simple, and, as spirits, unchanging in identity or form.

SOUL: 1. A special non-exportable American cuisine; 2. A type of music; 3. An individual entity that acts as the principle of life. According to Aristotle, the soul is the technical name of the substantial form of living beings.

SPECULATIVE: A type of knowledge that concerns itself with abstract concepts.

SUBJECT: A Latin word *sub-iectum,* which means "put under." The subject is the protagonist of acts. All acts require an acting subject. A subject acts upon an object, whether physical or intellectual (a known object, for example).

SUBJECTIVISM: This is a purely individualist view of the world from one's own perspective, without reference to the objectivity of things.

TENDENCY: See **APPETITE**.

TOLERANCE: From Latin *tollere,* to bear a heavy weight. A passive permission of a lesser evil. The very nature of the word affirms absolute truth, in that one permits an evil in order to avoid an

234 Common Nonsense *25 FALLACIES ABOUT LIFE . . . REFUTED*

objectively worse evil. Not that this is exactly the press the word "tolerance" is getting recently.

TRANSCENDENCE: Man is a spiritual reality. His spiritual nature is perhaps best exemplified by his longing for something more than himself, outside of himself. This longing is a fundamental structure of man, by which he incessantly goes out of himself and beyond the limits of his own reality, because, as spirit, he is naturally open toward the Absolute and attracted by It. This openness, which he implicitly affirms every time he knows any truth, or acts freely, is what we call spirituality. Man is spiritual; he lives his life in a continual tension between himself and the Absolute, in a constant openness to God. This is the condition that makes man what he is. As a spiritual being, man was made to fulfill himself in a spiritual way. Man's spirituality explains his spontaneous and natural openness to God.

TRANSCENDENTAL: See **TRANSCENDENCE**.

TRUTH: From the perspective of the Creator of all things, Who also knows all things, we can say that things are true because they are effects of His creating knowledge. Such truths are ontological truths. That's truth in the first sense. On the other hand, things are true when we know them, but they're not dependent upon our knowledge for their existence or ultimate truth. (That's why we can discover age-old truths every day for the first time.) In this second sense, truth is a meeting of the known thing and the knowing mind. What makes it possible for us to know an existing thing is its truth in the first sense, its ontological truth—the fact that it exists. Truth in the second sense, the act of knowing something, is logical truth, and the manifestation of this truth is yet a third kind of truth, the moment of certitude in which the logical truth is verified and accepted on the foundation of the ontological truth. It is interesting to note that there is also a moral truth that is a true moral norm that validly flows from moral principles. Just as in logical truth our minds (if they're thinking clearly) discover ontological truth, in moral judgment our wills (if their desires are ordered properly to our realization as human beings) conform to this moral truth.

UNCAUSED BEING: A being whose cause is itself. Instead of undermining the principle of causality, the existence of an Uncaused Being supports it. The principle of causality demands an uncaused cause (God) as the first cause of all other things.

UNIVERSAL IDEAS: Abstract concepts that exist logically (in your mind, the idea of a slug, for example) but not concretely (this slug in particular which I have raised from a pup, for example).

VICE: A habit that has a bad object.

VINCIBLE IGNORANCE: See **IGNORANCE**.

VIRTUE: A habit that has a good object.

WILL: A conscious tendency that is directed at an object proposed by the intellect. The intellect and the will work together, neither one being sufficient on its own for man to reach his goal. It's not enough for the intellect to know what dinner is: man has to use his will in order to feed himself. The will tends toward a known good.

WILLED IGNORANCE: See **IGNORANCE**.